How to Me
Interesting

Born in London in 1961, Gizelle Howard
spent her first few years in Pakistan. She
received bursaries to Farlington and later
Millfield schools, and has an LLB Hons (in
law). Among numerous 'character-building'
jobs, she has worked extensively abroad in
horse-racing and also at Saatchi & Saatchi
Advertising as a TV production assistant. She
left Saatchi's to write her first book *How to
Meet Interesting Men*. She is currently working
on two new books, and is based in London.

How to Meet Interesting Men

GIZELLE HOWARD

Mandarin

A Mandarin Paperback
HOW TO MEET INTERESTING MEN

First published in Great Britain 1991
by Mandarin Paperbacks
Michelin House, 81 Fulham Road, London SW3 6RB

Mandarin is an imprint of the Octopus Publishing Group,
a division of Reed International Books Limited

Copyright © Gizelle Howard 1991
Illustrations copyright © Amie Horse 1991

A CIP catalogue record for this title
is available from the British Library

ISBN 0 7493 1032 4

Typeset by Falcon Typographic Art Ltd,
Edinburgh & London
Printed and bound in Great Britain
by Cox & Wyman Ltd, Reading, Berkshire

Contents

Acknowledgements

First and foremost I would like to thank
my mother for her invaluable help
and support throughout the writing of
this book.

Thanks also to George Fontanini, Guy
Herbert, Adrian Lyons, Gerald Quinard
and David Sheridan who have all in
their different ways gone to considerable
lengths to assist me.

Lastly thank you to all those other people
who contributed their time, their ideas
and their entertaining stories to make this
book possible.

Author's Note

Neither the publishers nor I can be held responsible for any scrapes or difficulties that you get into as a result of reading this book. If on the strength of my advice you take up any adventurous and inherently dangerous activity such as hang-gliding, riding race horses or going on safaris, it is up to you to look after yourself – your life is in your hands!

In the same way, if you end up going to bed with any interesting man (or men) that you may meet as a result of reading this book, be very careful to protect yourself against sexually transmitted diseases – notably aids. The publishers and I cannot be held responsible for the consequences of your meetings. It is up to you to play safe in these matters. Your life is in your hands!

Introduction

An interesting man is a man who is interesting to you. He may be of any age, race, class or colour; he may be suave and sophisticated or sporty and debonair; he may be a worthy professional or a well-travelled bohemian, a farmer or a business man: whoever takes your fancy. He pleases you. He arouses your curiosity and appeals to you either sexually, emotionally, intellectually, spiritually, financially or otherwise. If he appeals to you on all of these levels then he is perhaps not only interesting but perfect as well!

Men and women usually restrict themselves to meetings within their social and working circles. Women frequently rely on two frail premises for finding an interesting man; chance and their looks. This book will put you into direct contact with new and interesting men who fall outside of these parameters, without you having to rely on chance or looks. Based on what I have learnt from interviewing many people the book suggests where to go and how to approach interesting men, without compromising your reputation!

Women from all walks of life complain that they don't, or can't, meet interesting men. Beautiful or glamorous women, women involved in fulfilling, absorbing careers, ladies of leisure and freedom – they, too, all ask the same question: 'How do I meet interesting men?' Attributes alone are not enough otherwise these fortunate women wouldn't be stuck for an answer. There is no shortage of interesting men as you will see later, but why do women find it a problem meeting them?

Firstly, there seems to be a fundamental distrust or an absence of a common language between the sexes. There is women's liberation on the one hand but many liberated, modern women have still not let go in their imaginations of the vestiges of the age of chivalry, where men used to woo their maiden sweethearts. They still strongly desire the 'perfect' man to appear from nowhere and to sweep them off their feet. Romance is, thankfully, still very much alive but many men do not want to continue laying their neck on the line and going through the gentlemanly conventions. Women are still unsure about the propriety of taking the initiative, seeing it as provocative or unfeminine or compromising or even coarse behaviour. Instead of opening up to men, and using their femininity, they so often end up disappointed with the traditional option of perching on the fence like a frosty bird, as of days of old, waiting for Mr Right to come along.

Taking the initiative doesn't mean the end of romanticism. It doesn't mean reversing roles. It doesn't mean chasing men. It simply means reassuring them of your interest from the beginning. It's selfish expecting guys to make all the effort. They are just as frightened of rejection as women, if not more so. Contrary to popular belief, men find it both refreshing and attractive if a woman takes it upon herself to break the ice, or if she responds positively to him in any given circumstances and takes it upon herself to ask him out. It is highly unlikely that she will ever be rejected. It doesn't mean that she is sexually available. It simply means that she would like to talk to him or to get to know him better – which is a charming proposition. See how it goes from there. Take a tip from a sophisticated and feminine woman I know, who is involved in the publishing world: 'I always call them the first two times. There is not much at stake at this point. If he doesn't take you up you can always say to yourself he's involved in another affair or he's terribly tied up with work.' Needless to say she has no shortage of interesting men to go out with!

The second obstacle to meeting interesting men is that not enough emphasis is attached to the fact that men and women complement one another in all ways: in the way they think, feel, see, behave and not only on a sexual level.

'Men are all only after one thing,' is a common reproach to this idea. Given the chance I don't think there are many men who would refuse a woman's entreaty into the bedroom, but that is not to say that they don't get along very well with her outside of the bedroom as well. Many men have developed extremely fulfilling relationships unwittingly with women who they may or may not have pursued further had it been left to them. In other words looks are by no means everything for those of you who are not self-confident regarding your appearance, and any man who is worth his salt will willingly admit this.

Notwithstanding falling in love, the greater the variety of men you endeavour to meet and understand, the more you will learn about yourself and about what you want from a man in the long term. When you meet your fantasy he may not live up to your expectations, but at least your curiosity will have been satisfied and you will be free to go on to explore new ground until you find what, or who, you are looking for. If you always seem to find yourself meeting the same type of men then I hope that this book will show you, realistically and unself-consciously, how you can meet interesting men from further afield. Otherwise I hope that it will encourage you to stretch your mind to try and appreciate those interesting men who are right under your nose. Plucking up the courage to take the initiative is obviously the key to solving the whole problem.

Imagine you are a lot older than you are now and looking down at yourself. What would you advise yourself to do? How many times do you hear older women saying, 'If I only knew then what I know now?' They probably weren't encouraged to meet interesting men – only eligible men. They certainly weren't encouraged to take the initiative. They didn't have the opportunities that we have now. They didn't recognise the power of women until they were caught up in family responsibilities and it was too late. The ball is now in your court. The interesting men are out there in their millions keenly awaiting word from you.

ONE

The Outdoor Type: Mr Lusty

An Attractive Proposition

Mr Lusty leads an adventurous life. You may find yourself on your way to foreign lands with him – perhaps off trekking in the Himalayas or canoeing around Corsica. Cash limitations and work may confine 'the action' to England – parachuting, hang-gliding, mountaineering, even environmental work. The bottom line is that he gets out of the house and into the open air on challenging escapades. You cannot fail to be inspired by this fresh, rugged soul.

He uses his initiative. He is courageous. He is self-sufficient. He challenges his physical strength and stamina in the context of real situations far removed from the likes of a body-building palace. His gutsy approach to life prepares him in the art of survival, so there is no question of you having to adopt the role of mother to him. You can be yourself.

On the Negative Side

Beware, adventure doesn't pay, unless he is a stunt man or prospecting for gold! His interesting history and exciting lifestyle are all too often founded upon a precarious bank balance. Keep an eye out for the wealthy ones unless, of course, you don't mind managing on a shoestring!

He is never at home. He is always out and about. In a relationship, this means that you either wait at home with baited breath for him to return from his daring escapades, or that you go with him. If you want to go with him don't be put off by his subconscious sexist excuses such as 'She isn't going to want to go larking on tough, shoestring holidays or gruelling treks.' What he means is 'I don't want a girl to slow things down or to get in the way of male business'. He may be right, especially if you have children, but surely you are the better judge of that.

The serious adventurer is not unduly preoccupied with women. He needs concentration in order to meet the physical challenges he sets himself in life, and so he needs to discipline his emotions. However, that is not to say that once he has found his life mate, he will not be romantic and ardent.

Social Tips

Mr Lusty, as a lover of the great outdoors, is not especially partial to trim social gatherings. He is often shy and retiring in formal situations, so you can't afford to be the society weed. Try to draw him out of himself by encouraging him to talk about his activities. Every one likes talking about themselves, it's the one subject we are all fond of, not least those who have something to talk about!

Lifting up the lid on Mr Lusty can reveal an Aladdin's cave of inspiring ideas. The morning after a Scottish Highland Spring Fling party in Bristol, my friend and I tentatively sat down on the lawn next to a shy, unassuming English man. He was silently staring with glazed eyes into his coffee, but before long we all drifted into conversation together. Soon he was recounting to us the ins and outs of a most exciting journey through Scotland that he had just made, culminating on a Brixham trawler sailing through the Outer Hebrides. By the end of breakfast, he had successfully persuaded both of us to go for a working holiday in Scotland as cook's assistants on one of the trawlers.

Mr Lusty thrives on challenging outdoor pursuits. There isn't the time for him to be unduly vain, nor as I have already said is there much time for women. Thus be ready to reassure him of your attraction, as did a good looking woman I know called Angela with Richard, a shy Welshman. They met at a dinner party in London. She was a glamorous woman working for Chanel; he was a boating, ornithology, and wildlife enthusiast. His outdoor pastimes immediately captured her imagination, and as Richard put it, 'Any one would have liked her because she was attractive and interested in what I was doing.' But not having much experience of women, he philosophically presumed her to be already taken up by 'loads of Nigel Porsches', and decided not to pursue the matter any further. The next day, the same party of people met at Hampstead fair. Keen to meet Richard on his own, Angela acquired his telephone number and invited him to another fair in Epsom later that week.

'You mean with the others?' he said.

'No, on your own,' she replied. One thing soon led to another and culminated in a passionate and wild affair on the Isle of Skye.

Sensibly Angela had taken the initiative. Richard's life, which was so far removed from hers, intrigued her. Unusually in such a situation it was the fact that apparently she had nothing in common with him which encouraged her to pursue him. In so doing she didn't let an interesting opportunity that was staring her in the face slip by!

Where to Find Mr Lusty

Cultivate an Adventurous Spirit

Put yourself in proximity with these men by cultivating an adventurous spirit. Take courage. Amongst the following examples are women who made a concerted effort to break from their blinkered world, instead of dwelling on the lack of excitement in their lives.

Parachuting

Parachuting, for me vertigo masochism, had always fired the imagination of Amanda. She was an ex-welfare counsellor who, at the time, was working in a famous London auction house. Although she liked her job, her social life was somewhat stale. She was bored of the company of the average art

3

world dandy with whom her work brought her into contact, and she was eager to meet someone more hunky!

Thus, she bravely tackled a **parachuting course** in order to introduce a new dimension into her life. The initial training was instilled over two evenings in a London hotel, at a cost of around £50. The fact that the men were as petrified as she was at the prospect of jumping from such a height helped to break down any barriers and inhibitions that might otherwise have existed between them.

The jump itself is the focus around which many hours may be spent waiting for suitable weather, and just as many hours afterwards trying to express the indescribable thrill and exhilaration of falling into the wide open air. It must give you quite a rush to find yourself still alive and having a drink afterwards!

Amanda described the experience as follows: 'The broad range of men was refreshing and made a great change of company. Although there was no social chitchat on what each person did, conversation was fluent and effortless so that I was able to be myself and relax. I didn't feel self-conscious or apologetic like I normally do. Learning to parachute was so exciting that I could think of nothing else.'

Before she knew it she had made friends with one of the guys on the course, and is now set up with his lusty best friend, a twenty-seven-year-old civil engineer!

Skiing
Nicola had been a single nurse for years and was anxious that she might end up as an old maid. 'Could I even survive out of uniform any more?' she wondered and took it upon herself to find out on the ski slopes. She had only been skiing once before but she had vivid memories of the fresh alpine air, the comfortable lifestyle, and the healthy, fit men. So, single, independent and adventurous, she gave up nursing and took a job as a ski chalet girl in the Italian Dolomites. Not unusually, while she was over there, she went out with a strong and graceful Italian ski instructor. He was so marvellous that she returned to Italy to teach English

over the summer. However, by then he had reverted to his trade as a carpenter, which didn't capture her imagination in the same way.

She returned to England. By now she was a fine skier as well as fluent in Italian. Most significantly she had gained a great deal of confidence. After one week she was hitched. She was introduced by one of the ex-chalet girls to a captivating university lecturer. He was a keen cyclist and climber, with whom she passed the best part of her time for a couple of energetic years!

Racing Stables

A great way to meet Mr Lusty is to work in a racing stables as a stable lass, i.e. exercising the horses. The book *Horses In Training* contains a list of trainers' names and addresses throughout the country. If you are tough, energetic and can ride, you stand a fair chance of surviving mentally as well as physically here. If you're not – forget it!

For me, the unpleasant experience of a rejection after a long relationship in England precipitated my dive into the French Newmarket, Chantilly. The experience built me up again, and made me see that there was a lot more to love in the world than I could ever dream of in the cocoon of my young, wounded heart – including French men!

The mêlée of wealth, speed, risk and beauty flushes out a toughness and sensitivity in the men involved in racing, notably the jockeys, stable lads and trainers, which is very exciting. Because there are relatively few girls in racing you will have an inexhaustible source of strong, daredevil men for the picking. Interesting characters abound. A delightful young French Bohemian described his life on a farmstead in Corsica, where he'd been living for the past four months. He showed me pictures of his trip to India the summer before. A Spanish trainer's son recounted his escapades at the August race meeting in San Sebastian.

There is always work available. Either call a trainer (see above) or simply go along to a racing centre such as Newmarket, Lambourne, or Newbury. You may like to go a little further afield, for example Chantilly near Paris or San Siro in Milan. Simply turn up at the stables and ask the head lad or trainer for work. You don't need to be as light as a feather, unless you want to race. Many men and women are seduced by the exhilaration and freedom this work affords. You can go as far afield as America, Australia, New Zealand, all over Europe, and land yourself a job at the drop of a hat. The experience brings you out of yourself and boosts your confidence no end. Once you have survived one innings it's a passport to almost anywhere in the world.

If you go abroad alone, the language barrier can only help relations with the racing society in which you find yourself. It obviously did for Rebecca, a cheerful and engaging twenty-six-year-old Lancashire lass. She had originally gone to work in Pisa just for the summer. Whilst over there she had met, and later moved in with, a wild and dashing Sardinian who rides in the Palio di Siena.

I was only at the standard of rusty O level French when I first arrived in Chantilly. I have spent many a ride trying to pronounce 'grenouille' which I still can't say! I didn't even know 'ciao' when later I went to ride in Italy. But I learnt soon enough for two reasons. As a girl in the racing industry you get filmstar attention, so there was an unending source of willing teachers. Secondly, due to an element of fear, I just had to learn. I frequently needed counselling on how to control my lively, pulling speed machine!

Flying Clubs

Flying jackets and Spitfires are, without a doubt, romantic images. If you go along to a flying club, (which you can find out about through the **Aircraft Owners & Pilots Association**, your Local Council or the Civil Aviation Authority) one sunny Saturday afternoon, you stand to meet some very interesting men of all ages and walks of life. *Pilot* and *Flypast* magazines usually have a programme of flying events for the year in their spring editions. By the way, you can usually count on the younger pilots being fairly wealthy.

Ask someone there, preferably a man, if you can watch or if there are any aerobatic displays during the afternoon. If there is a tea room, wander in and chat up any pilots who are sitting around. Introducing yourself will be simple if you just think of questions to ask him, such as where he's been or where he's going that day, if he does aerobatics or questions about the planes themselves. You could, for instance, enquire about a plane's history, or about the speed or distance it can withstand. He'll appreciate your interest without a doubt – I have heard aeroplanes are just the next step up from fast cars as penis extensions!

The Tiger Club in Headcorn in Kent specialises in bi-planes, notably the Tiger Moth. You can buy passenger membership for £40 per annum, which gives you access to all the club social events, as well as the opportunity to go for a joy ride now and again – maybe even abroad. Even without membership I am sure that you could wangle yourself a spin in one of the planes were you to go along one day out of interest and ask nicely.

But, a word of warning to those of you who would like to go out with a man interested in flying, from an engineer I met down there, 'Flying is a worse distraction than a mistress!'

Hot Air Ballooning
Sheila is an attractive computer analyst who I would describe as vital and enthusiastic; her most endearing feature is perhaps her sense of humour and bubbly laughter. She had a whale of a time meeting men whilst hot air ballooning at the weekends. Its wacky image, together with its fairy-tale associations, had always appealed to her. She seized the opportunity to crew one weekend for a man she'd recently met, and then she took the sport up seriously.

Like the parachutist above, she used the word 'refreshing' to describe the company, and greatly appreciated the friendliness between people without the need to know what everyone did in life. 'And yet with four to six in a basket you do get to know people! Added to which, a very important part of the day is the convivial drink in the pub afterwards, to chat over the day's happenings,' she commented.

Ballooning attracts a broad spectrum of people, from students to millionaires. It cuts right across the board both in terms of profession and age. Initial club membership – and there will almost certainly be more male members than female – is quite affordable but all in all it is an expensive sport. If you can't afford a flight but you want to be involved you can find crew work such as driving along behind in a car. Maybe they'll slip you in a flight!

You can get an idea of the crowd if you go along to the **Capital Balloon Club** which meets socially once a month in London's West End. I soon spotted a few interesting looking Mr Lustys! Contact the **British Ballooning and Airship Club** for details of meets around the country and abroad, as well as for club details.

Windsurfing

This is another male-dominated pursuit. It makes for well-made, outward-bound loners, striving for the harmony of balance and speed, pitted against wind and open water.

If you want to find the real professionals go for a walk along the beach on a rough, blustery day. In England this may mean challenging Atlantic coastal conditions. You won't have much competition. The chances are that it will be freezing cold and that you'll be the only one on the beach, so it'll be easy to start up a conversation. Offer to carry his board; he's probably exhausted and you'll want to warm yourself up. Then ask him if he'd like to go for a coffee. Alternatively, if you catch him going on to the beach in the morning, ask if you can wander down with him and maybe help him to carry something.

It's a fun interest to take up if you are in warmer climes because you are guaranteed to have numerous lithe males, either impressed and ogling, or just dying to help you! Isabelle, a pretty young English woman, started a summer romance this way. She was noticed struggling to stay up in the water by a strong, tanned, Greek law student. He offered her a hand and spent some time coaching her. From then on they were inseparable for the holidays.

Loulou, a busy career woman in her thirties, makes an effort every year to go abroad on a windsurfing holiday alone. She doesn't go looking for a man, I think she is more interested in her career, but the mini adventure opens up all sorts of possibilities for immediate introductions to a choice of hunky, clear-headed Mr Lustys.

Hang-gliding

Hang-gliding and microlight aviation (see **British Hang-gliding Association and British Microlight Aircraft Association**) are the source of a good many friendships and romances between men and women. Particular points of contact occur when help is needed to heave the hang-glider to the top of the hill. Once you have floated peacefully down to earth on your 'heavenly' flight you are bound to start chatting with the others who are waiting to go up themselves. You are welcome to give a hand, of course, even if you go along simply as a spectator.

Outdoor Clubs

Capable, outdoor Mr Lusty can be found in clubs involving other adventurous activities. Why not join him in learning to surf, fly, deep-sea dive, water-ski, row, pothole or canoe. An adventurous beautician I spoke to went out with her canoeing instructor for over a year. And if you are interested in a mountaineer but fear the climb, apart from the mountain side Mr Lusty can be found on the climbing walls of a numerous large Sports Centres!

All these activities give you plenty of room to be rescued as a damsel in distress. If, for instance, you take up rowing you may lose your oar which Mr Lusty will, hopefully, offer to retrieve. If you take up surfing, you may keep going under the waves rather than on top of them, so Mr Lusty will endeavour to take you under his wing and teach you to

9

master the art. He will always admire your perseverance. This is, of course, quite apart from introducing you to a new set of people naturally, instead of through the limitations of conventional socialising.

Club Mediterranee
Club Mediterranee is a comfortable compromise to the above specialised activities. It creates opportunities, in a holiday environment, to meet lusty, eligible, single men.

Go to Far Away Places
Get out, see and experience the world. It is stimulating to get out of an environment in which you are known, especially if you feel stale, unfulfilled, or have sad memories. A man who, like yourself, has got the character to get up and go to far away places, is by definition interesting. You'll make a great pair!

Men are attracted to women of character just as much as the other way round. You will return home with renewed confidence – a significant advantage if you are looking for Mr Lusty, but generally appreciated by most men. Having revived your flagging spirits you will be that bit more mature, and even stronger, to cope with suitors. In social situations your adventures will be an endless source of conversation and interest.

Bide your time in a remote corner of the world and Mr Lusty is almost bound to turn up. Better late than never, you can always extend your stay, or at the very least keep in contact with him. Out in the sticks he's going to treasure the contacts he has made, so make an excuse to return, even if it is only for a little holiday! A case in point is Jane, a beautiful, blonde physiotherapist who was working among Afghan refugees in Pakistan. After three months she fell in love with Alexander, a tough, aristocratic, English gem dealer on his way back from a mujaheddin hide-out across the border. Another example is Michaela, who after a year of teaching in a school in Zambia was joined by another teacher called Ian. He was a rugged and romantic, blue-eyed Irishman, who later became the love of her life.

Publications

Look for voluntary work abroad, such as picking coffee beans in Zimbabwe, in publications such as *Private Eye* and the *Guardian* — especially in June or July. Three excellent sources of information are *Overseas Jobs and Working Holidays*, the *Job Directory of Voluntary Work* and *Summer Jobs Abroad*. Work as a nanny or au pair within a family that has an outdoor lifestyle; perhaps on an Australian sheep farm or with a ski-orientated family in the Alps or Andes. They are bound to have friends with similar interests.

Courier

Fly far away economically. Contact a **courier company** in order to supplement the cost of flights on longhaul destinations to exotic places. You will be required simply to carry an envelope bearing customs paper work on the plane over. At prices such as £350 for a return flight to Rio de Janeiro, it puts adventure within your grasp. Half of the European flights cost as little as this. You may meet Mr Lusty on the journey, but if you don't there is time to search him out when you arrive.

It's not difficult to track Mr Lusty down in these wild, exotic destinations. Stay in youth hostels, or ask the locals about favourite English haunts. A tip for Peru, for instance, is to go to the one English pub in the country called the **Cross Keys** in the village of Cusco for a reliable source of adventurous men. A contact is all that you need to start on your quest for Mr Lusty. The British Embassy can always be of service too.

Expeditions

Expeditions are one of Mr Lusty's favourite occupations. If you would like to participate in one, contact the **Expeditionary Advisory Service**. It acts as a central database for planned expeditions, for all ages. Maybe you have specialist skills which could be used, like nursing or engineering, or maybe you want to pay for the ride in order to seriously search for red-backed tarantulas in Paraguay! Alternatively you may have to raise the sponsorship for a project yourself.

If you don't have the time or the money to go on an expedition, it is worth considering making an application for membership of the **Royal Geographical Society**. They have interesting lecture and film shows, at which there are many explorers and adventurers resting in between expeditions.

The geology or geography department of a university local to you will have information on expeditions that you can join, as a non-university member, or talks that you can attend. These will, of course, be packed with Mr Lustys. University anthropology and archeology departments will be able to direct you towards archeological digs. Here you will find outdoor thinkers!

Travelling

Backpacking and youth hostelling, whether at home or abroad, are one sure way to meet Mr Lusty. As you are all in the same rough circumstances, fellow backpackers are obvious targets for conversation. 'Where are you going?' or 'What are you doing here?' must be pretty standard lines of introduction!

Safaris

Look for work on a safari. They are an exciting haunt for Mr Lusty. You can obviously pay to go on a safari through a travel agent, but you might like to make it more of an adventure. The **Commonwealth Veterinary Association** has information on English vets working worldwide, some of whom will be working on safaris. They could sometimes use unskilled assistants.

Alternatively you could try your luck by turning up somewhere such as Tanzania or Kenya. Either contact the embassy directly for information, or go along to the nearest safari park there and offer your voluntary services, maybe cooking or doing odd jobs in return for your keep.

12

Overland Lorries

Overland lorries offer adventurous trips across wild terrain. Susie, a farmer's daughter, finding it difficult to meet anyone in the local farming community, went on one of these overland expeditions across Africa. She fell in love with the driver, who, rather typically, was an ex-public-school boy filling in time before university. They were married on their return to England. *Time Out* and most four-wheel drive magazines such as the *Land-Rover Owners International* magazine, frequently advertise these treks.

Countries with Outdoor Activities

Where there is an energetic, outdoor activity there is a lusty man to meet. Mr Lusty is particularly attracted to countries which abound in outdoor activities such as New Zealand. They offer bungey jumping – jumping off high structures on strong elastic cord – trekking, snow and jet-skiing, rafting, fishing and so on. Mr Lusty is attracted to splendid terrains such as South America with its spectacular mountainous landscape and fascinating ancient Inca civilisation. Contact the relevant embassies for details of activities their countries have to offer.

Sailing

A sailing man is attracted to travel and to the challenge of wrestling with the elements. I'd say, apart from the obviously unsettling nature of his activity, that he's a good bet. His sense of adventure, coupled with his vitality and vigour, make him an exciting proposition both physically and mentally. It has, however, been known for the stresses of sea life, together with the confines of a boat, to lead him to drink.

Beware that it takes a special relationship to survive the confines of a boat. You may admire competent, commanding men, but it doesn't always make for harmony when he's at the helm, bossing you around and or swearing at you. In other words, it's not for the faint hearted who cringe at bad language! To diffuse his superior position it is best to get to grips with the sport yourself, so that you are competent and assertive enough to work together as a team.

How to meet him
● Your most obvious bet is to find work on a boat. Able bodied people – cooks, au pairs, deck hands – are always needed, and although experience is preferable it is not essential. You just need to be healthy and energetic, at least in spirit. It is as well to know that many men will make allowances for your lack of experience, because they like the image of attractive or fun women on their boats. Yes, all right, the image is suspect, but it is nevertheless the truth!
● Wander around a sunny marina in the Mediterranean and look out for the British Ensign (flag) flying on the stern of the boats. Firstly ask on these boats if there is any work going. They tend to like English crew. It is always helpful if you have a grasp of another language, but it is not important. Look on a yacht club notice board for what jobs are on offer for working your passage. Put your own notice up – many do – indicating that you are looking for a working passage, for example from Nice – you may as well make sure he's wealthy in the process – to Palermo, Gibraltar or the Costa Smeralda!

Amanda, a twenty-five-year-old Australian, forged a plan of action in this vein, for the express purpose of meeting a suitable man. Fate and love at first sight were unforthcoming. She feared being left on the shelf, a frustrated spinster, looking after an ageing mother. As she put it, 'I decided that to meet interesting men, one had to go to where they hang out, preferably in great numbers, and where other females don't hang around them. Sailing seemed to fit the bill.' She trotted down to the local yacht club and put an advertisement on the notice board: Wanted. Small one-man dinghy. It would give her some experience of boats, albeit small ones, and at the same time it would give her a perfect pretext to make contact with those connected with yachts. She did not expect to meet someone so soon, but while putting the ad on the notice board, fate took the plan out of her hands. A great looking blond engineer came by and mentioned he wouldn't mind getting rid of the boat in his backyard. She duly went to have a look at the boat, took another look at him, and three years of love and fun together followed! So although her neat little plan was pre-empted, the principle was absolutely sound and she did learn to sail! As is often the case, once you are motivated into taking some positive action, the rest of life seems to fall into place.

But credit must be given as well to the little mongrel, Scrap, who she had picked up from the local dogs' home to join forces with her. She had acquired him because she thought that dogs help to break the ice when meeting people, which I think they definitely do as a source of interest or amusement. The blond hunk had a seductive, silky-coated sausage dog with him at the yacht club that day, to which Scrap took a great liking! This amusing scene of canine flirtation indeed sparked conversation and laughter.

● You can always pay for the experience of working along-side Mr Lusty on his boat. By living at such close quarters with a crew for two weeks you are bound to make friends, which builds up your chances of meeting people in the future! Two Laurel and Hardy characters built a magnificent catamaran in their local reservoir. When they had finished it they hadn't the experience to sail it outside of these confines. Not to be defeated, they placed an ad in a sailing magazine, offering to pay £50 a week in return for the experience of a working passage and some navigation lessons. They thus secured a trip on a boat heading across the Atlantic to the West Indies.

● Navigation courses will bring you into direct contact with Mr Lusty without you even having to go to sea. You can find out about these through the **Royal Yacht Association** or a yachting magazine. Alternatively, join a sailing school by the same route. Kay, an outgoing hotel management trainee decided to do a navigation course over a year of evening classes. She was the only woman on the course and thoroughly enjoyed herself. Following that she got a job as a cook on a sailing boat in The Half Ton Cup race, where she met a lusty chartered surveyor. Sailing holidays in exotic surroundings, weekends in Paris, expensive presents, all manner of indulgence followed.

● You will find Mr Lusty in harbours and marinas. He is usually to be found tinkering around on his boat. Engage him in conversation by admiring and enquiring about his pride and joy. With the neverending movement of boats, either on their way to, or from somewhere, these places could be described as social playgrounds. Don't be surprised, therefore, if you are spoilt for choice amongst all those men. It's not a bad thought!

● Cowes week on the Isle of Wight, in the first week of August, is the high point of the sailing set's social calendar. It is an exciting eight-day pageant of boat racing, from pram dinghies to ocean racers, which is set off by a great deal of partying for thousands of crew and spectators! If you want to join in the fun you should book accommodation well in advance in either Cowes itself, in East Cowes or, for example, in the nearby village of Gurnard. The **Cowes Tourist Information Centre**, which is open from Easter, will be able to assist you, but they strongly advise you to book as early as possible.

Environmental Work

Don't be put off from giving the following activities further thought. A broad spectrum of interesting Lusties, ranging from professional men to cultural leaders, are attracted to them.

The great thing about involving yourself is that even if you don't meet the man of your dreams straight away, you are nonetheless motivating yourself. You are generating energy. You are exposing yourself to a greater range of people and building up contacts. Surely you have to be better off switching on the life inside you than vegetating in front of a soap opera!

The following story is typical of the kind of unsuspected meeting that occurs when a number of new people come

16

together to work on a physically demanding project. Sally's company, previously helped out of difficulty by Scott Badars Quaker Cooperative, was now returning the favour to other fledgling companies. This involved a working weekend to help ailing miners, suffering from lung disease and disabilities, to improve their factory and production line for the manufacture of storage heaters. Ten years ago she met Oliver here, a thirty-four-year-old divorcee father of one, who was helping through another organisation on the same project. He became the love of her life. Subsequently they sailed away on a romantic voyage to North Africa, on a boat that Oliver had spent four years building.

The National Trust has many interesting projects, such as refurbishing old croft houses in Scotland. To participate in one of these projects costs in the region of £90 a week, including travel, food and board. Despite the fact that you will probably need to take your longjohns and gum boots, and pass the occasional tea break sheltering with the others from the rain, it is from all accounts a delightful way to meet Mr Lusty.

See address section for examples of outdoor charity organisations in addition to:

World Wildlife Fund For Nature UK and International. Their voluntary work is mainly fund raising. **Citizens Advice Bureau**; they can always give information on environmental clubs and courses going on in the locality, eg the Open University countryside course. **British Trust For Conservation Volunteers** (BTCV); they arrange voluntary, outdoor urban work such as canal clearance and tree plantation. **The Natural Break** is run by them as well. This organises over four hundred conservation working holidays for a nominal price of £30 per week including board and lodging, and £10 for a weekend.

Why not organise a sponsored activity such as abseiling down your local church spire, or a petanque competition in order to raise funds for a charity such as Greenpeace? Afterwards you could organise a party for the lusties who have turned up.

Farming

Mr Lusty the farmer could enter like a breath of fresh air into your life. Both categories of farmers, those with small and those with large farms, are attractive propositions. Farmers with smaller farms offer the cosy scenario of the countryside, isolation and a picturesque farmhouse. Your love is always near at hand, although perhaps a little too near! It's also a paradise for children. It's obviously ideal if you are partial to animals and wish to live the outdoor life. On the down side, there are few, if any, holidays and times can be hard. Frequently you are completely tied to the farm, especially if there is livestock. With the farmers of large farms you can be assured of wealth! But unless you are keen on mucking in, or mucking out, pick a gentleman farmer who won't expect you to drive a tractor, and who will still take holidays like anyone else.

● Ways to meet him. Agricultural colleges are the best venue in which to meet young farmers. The ratio of men to women is always tremendously in your favour. Why not consider attending one of their courses. As well as the full-time one- and three-year courses, which usually run from nine to five, five days a week there are also, for example, the nine to five day releases or evening courses. Note that some of the courses may be only loosely based on agriculture.

Melissa, a forty-year-old divorcee who had been deserted by her husband and left with two kids, brightened up her life considerably by attending an agricultural course. Her children were at school during the day. Single-mindedly, she left Scotland for a well known agricultural college in the south west of England and took up a course on environmental management, a subject in which she only had a very vague interest. Within weeks she was fixed up with a wealthy, young, twenty-year-old toyboy!

● Agricultural colleges of high repute hold splendid college balls where not a penny is spared. You can either apply directly for a ticket or you can obtain one from a sympathetic member of college staff, or from one of the students. Because of the lack of female students women are naturally always popular. Tickets nonetheless go fast, so it is advisable to apply for one in advance.

● If you are interested in the very wealthy farmers, the *crème de la crème* are to be found at the **Cirencester Royal Agricultural College**. Other particularly wealthy colleges are **Seale Hayne** in Devon, **Wye** in Wales, **Harper Adams** in Newport, **Writtle** in Chelmsford and **Askam Bryan** in York.

● The **Young Farmers Club**. Most rural areas have got a branch of the YFC. There are actually quite a few female members but again the ratio is male biased. Surprisingly, as long as you express some interest in farming, you don't have to be a farmer to join. One of the main purposes of the club is for socialising by means of barn dances, discos and dinners, particularly in the winter.

It was at a barn dance that Caroline, who had just started working for an estate agent, met her future husband. She went along to a barn dance for the first time, and split her skirt whilst climbing over a fence in order to get to the loo. She had to run home and change. All she could find to wear was a very short and pretty mini-skirt! She was spotted straight away by an admiring farmer, her future husband, who promptly offered her a drink. A lesson to be learned from that story is that if you don't make an impression the first time around, accidentally on purpose spill something on your dress. You then have the perfect excuse to run home and return wearing the sexiest thing you can find!

It was at a YFC dinner at a local hotel that nineteen-year-old Jackie met her millionaire farmer, future husband. He has kept her in clover ever since. Among other luxuries she is indulged in exotic holidays twice a year, and encouraged to drive his Lamborghini car whenever she wants to!

● Look for work on a farm as a groom, or for work as a pupil, in order to gain experience before going to an agricultural college. These sort of jobs are advertised in the back of *Farmers Weekly* and *Horse and Hound* magazines. It doesn't matter if you give up the idea of the college, especially if you are swept off your feet by a strong and loving Mr Lusty! I became friends with a couple of students from the local agricultural college whilst working in the strawberry fields one summer for extra cash. They were gaining practical experience and, in the process, stuffing themselves with strawberries!

- Market days obviously attract farmers in their hordes. You won't have much female competition here, if any, so you are sure to turn a few heads. Have a look around. Ask anyone who takes your fancy questions about where he comes from, what kind of farming he does, what is the most popular sort of farming in that area. He will be responsive because it's so unusual and such a sweet relief to have a woman at hand. He's down to earth and is unlikely to demur at the chance to show you around his farm.

- A divorcee mother of three took up an unusual job for a woman, selling fertilisers to farmers in the Hampshire area. She made a number of interesting encounters and ended up living with one of her former customers.

- County shows are another appropriate venue for Mr Lusty. An excuse to talk to him may be to admire his pretty Charolais cow, or to ask him if you could take a picture of his shire horse!

- Point-to-points and hunt meets are excellent occasions for meeting Mr Lusty farmer. You are sure to find him amongst his friends in the beer tent. Dates and locations for these are to be obtained from the local newspaper.

Farmers don't generally come into contact with many women so don't hesitate to grab your opportunity when it presents itself. James, a twenty-seven-year-old farmer, gave a dinner party and invited one particular acquaintance and his girlfriend. The girlfriend was quite taken by her host and cunningly wrote to thank him for the party. She rounded off her letter with, 'Should you invite me again I'd be most willing to come down.' He subsequently did invite her. In fact she went down frequently at the weekends from then on, and a year later they were married.

Lynn was a trendy, thirty-two-year-old TV editor who had recently separated from the man in her life. She had

20

had enough of men for the time being. They were the last thing on her mind. One weekend she went down to her mother's house in a remote village in the Cotswolds. Her mother told her about Paul, the next door farmer who had just split up from his wife and children, and who was thus depressed. Together they decided to pay him a neighbourly visit. Perhaps because of their similar circumstances Lynn and Paul hit it off immediately. On her return to Bristol, Lynn thought a lot about him. Aware of his isolation and his strained financial circumstances she took the initiative and invited him to dinner, which, incidentally, she paid for as he was so skint, at a half-way point between his home and Bristol. They built up a relationship over the winter weekends, and now her permanent weekend home is his house in the Cotswolds.

Having been let down by her fiancé, Fiona returned to her rural family home to nurse her aching heart. After a few months a friend of hers eventually managed to persuade her to go out to a local pub darts evening. She had agreed to go, albeit grudgingly, so she couldn't easily back out when she learnt about her friend's plan to introduce her to Gerald, a farmer in the district. She didn't go overboard about him when she met him and they parted without exchanging numbers, or even surnames. Gerald, however, had taken quite a fancy to her, and being young and enterprising, quizzed her local village Post Office mistress to find out her address and telephone number. He called her up and asked her out. She graciously accepted his invitation. He turned the tables in his favour because Fiona soon married him. Gerald is a dairy farmer, and Fiona has her own chiropodist's business. Her father was particularly delighted with the match. Being in the insurance business, he had always advised her to 'Marry a farmer because he'll be rich through inheritance!'

The Forces
The Visit-new-places-meet-interesting-people gang from the Army fall into the Mr Lusty category, as do those in the Navy, the Marines and the Air Force.

His well-respected career can guarantee you security, simply because any particular service in the forces is the biggest family you'll ever get. That apart, he's intensely masculine and endowed with a body in as perfect nick as his uniform. He is taught to be decisive, protective and honourable. He may be so honourable in fact that you need to reassure him with a 'first move'. On the other hand, once he's reassured, from all accounts he is sex mad!

What more could you ask for? Well, imagination and originality are not encouraged. Those in the forces are there to obey orders! That is not to say that you won't be smuggled in and out of back windows during the early days! You must enjoy travel as you usually have to pull up roots every couple of years. I have been told by a reliable source that although many service homes are in civilian areas, life for a woman in parts of the forces can become claustrophobic where service accommodation is provided in the garrison. Here, however, is an ideal situation for a woman who enjoyed the position of monitor or head girl at school. The institutional rules will not bother her and she will be able and willing to involve herself in activities such as the Wives' Club.

How to meet him
• Army officers.   At the top end, their wide range of tough physical activity is rounded off with polo, skiing and shooting. Officers will welcome new faces. The point is that for all their virility, officers have a hard time meeting girls, or at least they have a hard time sustaining a relationship because of the rigorous army regime. Their situation is not helped by the fact that as young, up and coming officers at, for example, Military Academies, they are not encouraged to marry young. Traditionally, army officers are not supposed to marry before they are twenty-five.

The usual way to meet an officer, or future officer, in any of the forces, is to obtain an invitation to a regimental ball, eg the Army Staff College Ball in Camberley in June or the unit of Territorial Army Artillery Company Annual Flank Company ball in Finsbury Square, London at the same time. An invitation to an army ball can of course be secured at a snooty society drinks party in fashionable districts such as Windsor or Chelsea. You can just as easily obtain one by asking an officer's friend or sister if you can be invited along to the next officers' party. If you have been invited once you will most surely be invited again. Many city gents are members of the unit of Territorial Army Artillery Company and are thus a good target for securing an invitation. However, bear in mind that most TA members are away on camp at the weekends so if you want to spend any time with him you may have to join him!

No expenses are spared at these lavish occasions, where dinner is cleared away with the military precision of a silent troop of ants, and finished off with coffee on silver trays — quick march! Then it's the bouncy castles and coconut shies to keep the passion for activities rolling. Every army regiment has its peculiar customs. At one Highland regiment ball I went to they danced wild Highland reels and insisted on only opening the champagne with razor sharp Claymore swords.

Be careful about dress. The Army mess kit is very glamorous with gold frogging, a monkey jacket, tight trousers (so, ladies, you may be tempted to pinch his bottom) and spurs! You should be very glamorous as well but at the same time you must be careful not to upstage the army wives by wearing too skimpy a mini-skirt or too revealing a see-through blouse, for instance. You must be aware of customs. Look non-plussed or nonchalant and take it all as it comes, ie behave as though you are used to this scene. As with everything, coolness creates more of an impression. If you get bored with your partner there is no shortage of alternative men to chat up or to be chatted up by.

Travelling and adventure will engage a good deal of hearty conversation. You would be right to ask where Mr Lusty officer has been posted before, where he is going, if he likes travelling, what sort of adventures he has experienced. He'll be dying to show you his war wounds and his photo album of adventures!

You will find that, despite the regimental discipline, the Sloane accents and the manic need for organisation, officers

23

are for the most part extremely thoughtful, positive, and tough, with an innate or highly schooled sense of courage and adventure. But you will need to enquire into their activities, because invariably 'wine, women and song' are the purpose of the gathering. You may find some of the officers off-putting because of their extrovert nature.

● Naval officers.   Naval officers have an outgoing, interesting life, but they may be called away to sea for long periods of time during which you will be left on your own. Popular haunts for naval officers are of course pubs and sailing clubs around the main naval bases of Portsmouth, Plymouth and Rosyth. I have been told that the Barbican area in Plymouth and the Grass Market area in Edinburgh are popular with naval officers.

At the Royal Navy Engineering College in Manadon near Plymouth there are nearly four hundred up and coming naval officers undergoing a three-year training course, so you shouldn't have much difficulty finding fresh, eligible Mr Lusties around here! Dartmouth, home of the British Royal Naval College is another hot spot for up and coming naval officers. Their summer and Christmas balls take place in the local village and have been described to me as 'idyllic', so it might be worth trying to get yourself invited!

When you do meet a naval officer, suggest that you would like to go to one of the naval balls. I am sure he will be able to assist you. Alternatively, try writing a polite letter to one of HMS ships' commanding officers for an invitation to a ball. This could well be the ticket!

When foreign war ships visit English ports the naval attachés attached to the various embassies usually lay on a welcoming party for them. They get many of their female party recruits from local universities but they are always on the look out for more. You could enquire around some of the embassies — American, Russian, Italian — whichever nationality takes your fancy. The parties are usually held on board a ship and are glamorous, exciting occasions with lots to drink. Go easy, though. I hear that the married Lusties of the foreign ship's company are often the most pushy while

24

the single men are often more shy and hang back a bit, so take your time to study the form!

• Marine officers.   Their lifestyle is much the same as naval officers with travel and variety. They are used to being called away at short notice and working odd hours. It is not a nine-to-five job! Their everyday social haunts are local pubs, clubs and discoteques.

One of the most sure, although remote, places to find marine officers is in the area around the Marine Commando Training Centre of Lympstone near Exeter. Officers all belong to a mess where they eat, often sleep and socialise. Quite apart from the summer and Christmas balls they have informal do's and parties. Some enterprising women have been known to successfully introduce themselves to these men by writing to the officer's mess secretary for an invitation to a mess ball or party, in order to meet some new people. This isn't appropriate in all services and messes because of the security aspect but it is certainly worth a try. The main marine ports are Taunton, Plymouth, Arbroath, Poole and Portsmouth.

• RAF officers.   RAF officers have a glamorous image which is very appealing to women. They are dispersed amongst about a hundred and twenty, often very isolated, bases around the country. Lincolnshire and Norfolk probably have the greatest concentration. Bases such as Brize Norton and Lyneham near Oxford are more well-known bases. They, too, lead a social existence in the local area and in whichever mess they belong to. Dinner nights, informal parties and summer and Christmas balls, commonly known as draws, are popular forms of recreation. You could find out about RAF bases local to you in the telephone directory.

You are sure to meet RAF officers at air shows. A good opening line to one of the pilots that day would be to say that you very much enjoyed watching his display and then to ask him about himself, where he works, when he will be doing a display again and so on. Flattery is a sure bet – always!

• Other ranks.   It is more difficult to pinpoint where to

meet other ranks in the services except through bars, discos and pubs in the garrison towns such as Aldershot and Colchester for the Army, Plymouth for the Royal Navy, Exmouth for the Marines and Boscombe Down or the remote outposts of Locking or Coltishall for the Royal Air Force.

Outward bound leisure activities.

Lusty outdoor activities have increased in popularity in recent years. Paint ball games have a Yuppy image but they do draw from a wide social spectrum. The game consists of two teams, shooting it out in the countryside, with compressed air guns firing harmless paint bullets. By all accounts it is a tremendous day out for both men and women, who, incidentally, often do better at it than men, an opportunity to really let go. You could always pin Mr Lusty down at gunpoint when you take him prisoner. Paint ball games cost in the region of £35 per day, and can be located through most shooting magazines. See **Mayhem Wargames Ltd**.

The English Civil War Society organise weekends all over the country in which people of all ages and types can participate in re-creating historical events. They may, for instance, re-enact a civil war battle, or rather a couple of hours of battle. The rest of the time is spent socialising in seventeenth-century garb in the local hostelry! It has been described to me as 'glorified camping and hearty fun' and more seriously as 'recreating living history'. Apart from the possibility of being swept off your feet by a dashing young Royalist cavalry officer, you may more than anything else enjoy experimenting with a new wardrobe!

A very attractive aspect of this type of activity is that it brings people of diverse occupations and backgrounds — computer engineers, army officers, shop workers and wealthy city whizz kids to mention but a few — together in a relaxed and stimulating environment.

TWO

The Intellectual Type: Mr Worldlywise

Wise and worldly intellectuals who are interested in knowledge, enlightenment and the quality of life are featured in this chapter. With this quote in mind – 'Life is a comedy to those that think, and a tragedy to those that feel' (Horace Walpole) – I would describe his life as a mixture of both!

An Attractive Proposition

Perhaps Mr Worldlywise's most compelling attribute is that he values his girlfriends so highly. To him manly protection extends beyond the physical and out to his protective concern for her independent development as a person. He is passionate about her. Antonio, an Italian intellectual I know, is a particularly good illustration of this point, because of the male chauvinist society in which he lives. Monique, a vivacious, forty-two-year-old English business woman, who was more interested in maintaining a high standard of living than being tied down by the bonds of marriage, met Antonio whilst working in Rome. He was a university professor of micro-biology and unlike most of his compatriots he was in no way chauvinistic. In due course she married him. Her reasons for doing so were, 'He gave me so much faith, he gave me so much freedom. He was terribly concerned for my own good.' It wasn't because she had discovered love for the first time, nor because she was fascinated by his subject!

Mr Worldlywise holds love in high regard. We are all selfish but he seems to be particularly alive to his partner's needs, and to the importance of concerning himself with them. After all, he is thoughtful!

29

All the Worldlywises to whom I have spoken truly believe in equality between men and women, without detracting from their appreciation of femininity. In other words in a relationship they wouldn't feel threatened by a clever, successful, thinking woman, because they are generally intelligent enough to realise that they are not in competition with her. This is a change from many men I have come across, who have made it clear that they would prefer to have a relationship with a woman who was not quite as clever as them. That's as bad as being turned down from a job because you are over qualified. I suppose they have old fashioned notions of being in command of a relationship, which leaves little room for love, and leads you to read books like *How To Meet Interesting Men*! Despite my understanding of their insecurity, I have little sympathy with their attitude in these enlightened times.

Quality of life and freeing the spirit emerge as Mr Worldlywise's paramount considerations, following from which he should prove supportive about any project you might want to attempt, as did this Worldlywise fellow.

On his return from Ethiopia, Jeremy, a well travelled Glaswegian doctor in his forties, took over a small country practice. Following a family tragedy he became an alcoholic and was supported sympathetically throughout this appalling period by Sarah, a freckled and curly haired nineteen-year-old barmaid who worked downstairs. The surgery was strategically located over the local village pub! On his recovery they married, and he repaid her kindness by encouraging her to train as a doctor. Upon qualifying she returned several years later to take over his village practice, while he went on to become a specialist.

Many Worldlywises have earned a cushy lifestyle for themselves, although by nature they are seldom preoccupied with acquisition. There is also the prestige and security of their position in society to be considered.

Mr Worldlywise is stimulating company and by definition his mind will remain lucid and vital. This is both an inspiration and a great tonic for keeping you young. After chatting for over five hours to a middle-aged Worldlywise solicitor, it was uplifting to leave feeling as though I had been talking to some one in his twenties. His thoughts were so fresh and alive. He must certainly keep his wife on her toes, although she is, from all accounts, equally vital, involved in national tennis championships, the writing of newspaper features as well as the organisation of numerous charity events. She is a great fan of Harley Davison motorbikes too!

Given the fact that Mr Worldlywise is prone to the exchange of ideas, he keeps interesting company. He has an eclectic mixture of friends from all walks of life, among whom there are numerous articulate and artistic ones. The so called 'intellectual' parties which I have attended have always been buzzing occasions of excess and hilarity. If you get fed up of your original Mr Worldlywise, remember that there will be no shortage of interesting alternatives. Watch out though, because the same goes for him if he tires of your company!

Mr Wordlywise is not always preoccupied with intellectual discussion but there is the pleasure of knowing that he is always receptive to it. Following a long discussion one Sunday afternoon with a *Financial Times* journalist over my book, I was asked back a little later to take part in a backgammon tournament – which incidentally I won! The most intellectual we got was to ask 'Should we go to Sarah's so that we can play in the garden?' Admittedly we had all had a few glasses of wine!

On the Negative Side

Because his mind is so active he may be truculent, argumentative, and, at times aggressive. He may talk too much and too intensely, which can become tiring – and boring!

The other side of Mr Worldlywise's coin of love and understanding may well be rational infidelity! As one of my married Worldlywises' rules of thumb goes: You should respect and like the affairee, but you must always make it clear that you love your wife. Don't be unfaithful if it makes

31

you feel guilty. Don't talk to anyone about it. Don't tell all to your wife in a fit of honesty to get it off your chest. It's your responsibility!

Some Worldlywises may not be aggressive enough, a bit 'newmannish', which may get on your nerves. He may think too much, even during sex!

Notwithstanding the above points, all in all he is an attractive proposition. His way of looking at life could do you wonders. And, if you don't like it, he is open to persuasion to be shown otherwise!

Don't be Intimidated

Don't feel intimidated by what you interpret to be Mr Worldlywise's all consuming intelligence. You don't have to be an artist to appreciate an artist nor do you have to be an intellectual to appreciate an intellectual. George, a kindly, self-effacing tutor, recounted how women often felt intimidated by him. He described a typical introduction at a party:

Her: What do you do?
Him: Uhm, I teach. What do you do?
Her: I'm a secretary. What do you teach?
Him: Philosophy of law . . .
Her: That's interesting. (She thinks, Oh boy, that's the end of that conversation!)

It doesn't have to be like this. If you're curious about what makes a man tick, you should have no problems. The only thing that you know about George is that he is a Philosophy of Law tutor. What about the rest of his life? What sort of life does such a man lead? The conversation can be continued: 'That's very interesting but it must be quite tiring. What do you do to relax . . . ?' or 'Why don't you practise law instead of teaching it?' or 'Have you always lived in this part of the world?' – anything to bring the conversation on to neutral ground. Mr Worldlywise has just as big an ego as anyone else, so he likes talking about himself.

Mr Worldlywise is interested in people for what they are,

and is not looking for a Mrs Einstein. In fact he often gravitates to a quite level headed kind of woman whose practical sense brings him down to earth. George, who described the above dialogue, is, for instance, married to a welfare officer. You just need to keep an open mind and to allow yourself to be engaged in thought and enquiry from time to time without clinging obstinately to narrow minded preconceptions of life.

If you are ever really stuck for something to say try the humorous approach. Mr Worldlywise appreciates wit. I know a Dutch Worldlywise who is liable to throw the following kind of line at a party of new people hoping for a lively response: 'What do you think is the most erotic part of your body?' Such a question might ruffle the fastidiousness of an English Worldlywise, but one sure way of drawing him out of his shell and of interesting him will be humorous debate!

What to do with Intellectual Snobs

Regrettably you will inevitably encounter the occasional intellectual snob. The problem is what to do with him. Too much deferential agreement with him is likely to bore rather than to encourage. Probably it is best to ignore him. Justify his obnoxious character by telling yourself that he probably only knows a lot about one thing, and is trying to make up for his little willy! Intelligence is abstract and separate from the person. It may be an admirable and challenging attribute, but it's not in any way the measure of a person's worth. Mr Worldlywise knows as well as anyone that it's not what you know that is important so much as the process by which you arrive at your conclusions. If only more men understood that!

Where to Find Mr Worldlywise

Travel and the Arts
Mr Worldlywise is a ubiquitous individual drawn to travel and the Arts. Details of how to meet him in these situations are set out in Chapter Six, the Arty Type, and Chapter Eight, the Travelling Type.

Higher Education

Put yourself directly into an intellectual environment, either by taking a degree yourself as a young student, or as a mature student. Naturally many loves blossom at university or polytechnic, not least because everyone there is interacting and developing together. In a normal job the mind is often quiescent, if not stagnating, and fewer people are encountered. Particularly a little later in life, when your social network may appear closed, higher education offers the opportunity to come out of yourself and to mix unselfconsciously amongst new blood and new brains!

Jill, a young English literature graduate, told me how she secured a meeting with the object of her desire at university, an earnest young man with a bit of a stammer. On realizing that he was too shy to have ever asked her out, she stuck a note on his car windscreen: If you'd like to come along to a party this evening, I'll be at my house until seven pm. Find Jill. He didn't hesitate to knock on her door that evening, and they went out together for the rest of their time at university.

Don't despair if commitments or lack of funds don't allow you to take up a full- or part-time degree. What you may not realise is that on most college notice boards there are details of activities open to non-students as well. Visit a college and look out for open lectures on popular subjects of intellectual interest.

When at one of these lectures, show your face a few times so that Mr Worldlywise grows accustomed to it. If you are alone, it may be a good idea to park yourself next to a solitary man in the lecture theatre. While you are about it choose the most attractive man there! Strike up conversation by asking if you can borrow a pen or something. Always remember that men greatly appreciate it if a woman helps to break the ice initially. You would be surprised how many opportunities have been missed because of shyness on the man's part.

Another way into a university/polytechnic is to go to their canteen at a quiet time of day for a coffee, preferably with a friend. Park yourself next to one of the guys and find out what he's studying, and whether he enjoys life there. Ask

34

with a view to taking up a course yourself. If his own course interests you, ask if perhaps you could go along to one of the lectures with him. If you would like to do something else ask him to point you in the right direction. It is all food for conversation. You can use the same approach in the library although you must be sensitive to people studying. Don't underestimate the number of friendly meetings that have taken place behind the book shelves either!

Lecturers

Intelligence and power are considerable attractions. The implied intellectual superiority of a lecturer, coupled with his teaching expertise, are a great turn on to some women.

You don't want to cause too much of a rumpus at your college, so be discreet. Drop back after lectures on some pretext or excuse. Yasmin, an exotically beautiful Egyptian woman, met her International Studies lecturer, an articulate man in his early thirties, at a cocktail party. He took her fancy so she stopped back after a lecture the following week and invited him to her dinner party. She thought that the worst he could do was refuse, but needless to say he found it difficult, as men do! A passionate affair ensued so what more could she have asked for? Well, perhaps she would have liked the affair to last a little longer. Unfortunately he was concerned by what he considered to be her bourgeois mentality and one evening it got the better of him. His passion died completely when she returned from a holiday in Switzerland and whispered to him, 'When I made love with Hans [that was her affluent, official Swiss boyfriend] all I could think of was you!'

Alternatively, if you do start a relationship with one of the lecturers whilst at the college, avoid having any academic involvement with him. Chloe, a pretty but retiring brunette, having fallen in love with a biology lecturer, or rather with his deep, mellow voice, was stuck as to how to actually meet him. She rejected her friend's advice, to simply go up and talk to him in the canteen, due to an understandable lack of courage! The same friend therefore successfully took the matter into her own hands. She invited Chloe to join her and the biology lecturer over lunch, and then left them alone at a pertinent moment. The relationship blossomed from there for the rest of the degree course.

Perhaps the best piece of advice I can give is to avoid getting involved with your tutors or lecturers when at college, but to remain in contact, or to resume contact at a later date, once you have left. That way they don't have to compromise their professional responsibilities. However, when you do leave, there is no reason not to bring any latent attraction into the open. It is a good idea to keep lecturers and tutors as friends in any case. They may be the only source of intellectual contacts that you have once you find yourself in the outside world!

University Towns
Look for work in university towns such as Oxford or York. In order to place herself in a stimulating environment Karen, a twenty-seven-year-old school matron from Whitney, secured a post in a boy's prep school in Oxford. She went out of her way to meet Mr Worldlywise in clubs, societies and debates. Eventually she met David, a golden-voiced thirty-five-year-old geography lecturer, after joining a university college choir. So successful was their meeting that they ultimately lived together.

Work in Higher Education
Alternatively, find temporary work in a university or polytechnic. Nineteen-year-old Christine fell in love with one of the lecturers from the polytechnic legal faculty in which she was temping. In order to ensure that she met this man again she firstly renewed her contract there several times, and then bought a ticket for the college Law Society dinner. Whilst dancing with him, at her request, she declared, "I'd really like to be making love with you right now, in bed". Well, that was one way of taking this interesting man's breath away, as well as provoking an interesting debate for the night ahead on the morals of her declaration!

Identify Yourself with a Cause

Mr Worldlywise is one of a rare breed who has strong principles and believes in sticking to them. Consequently he is to be found actively participating in support of a good cause. A common goal towards which people are working together is a perfect climate for fostering relationships. For example, picketing until three am you get to know people as they really are, which can be hilarious and a kind of freedom in itself. Long hours and sometimes trying conditions bring down barriers and allow people to see one another in their true light – with and without make up, feeling good and under stress. At least this gives you a chance to judge the whole album rather than just a snapshot, because often, as I discovered when I was interviewing these men, first impressions are never enough to convey the complexity of a person's character.

If you participate in one of these events be careful! Michael, a nuclear-disarmament campaigner, and his future fiancée, were picked up by the police together and thrown in separate jails for a few days. Such an unpleasant experience is to be avoided although in their case the fear and excitement precipitated a mutual admission of love, or lust, the moment they were freed!

On one occasion I went with a couple of girlfriends to interview people who were rallying outside South Africa House. Some mindless idiot threw red paint at the Embassy, but half of it landed on my face and all over my clothes. I looked as if I was covered in blood and so created quite a stir. As usual I made friends when I was fully occupied and least expecting it. On my way for comfort and help at the home of an ex-boyfriend who was in town, I was befriended by a sympathetic, and incidentally not bad looking, American tourist. Instead of staring aghast at me as did everyone else on the tube, he asked me what had happened. He contacted me the next day and there followed a few dinners and a trip to Salisbury Plain together. Now I have an open invitation to stay with him in America. One of the men who I had interviewed earlier was also concerned for my welfare. He took the trouble to find my telephone number and called me at work the next day. He is an active member of an anti-apartheid group and works in the legal profession. Since this time we have passed many hours together.

Such controversial causes attract Worldlywises from many walks of life, including artists, lawyers, teachers and students. You may, for instance, find yourself alongside a Mr Worldlywise making placards, preparing food or reporting events.

Politics
Mr Worldlywise is often involved in politics. Lawyers especially fall into this category, so if you are able to muster sufficient interest, you will be well advised to join, for example, your local Conservative, Liberal, Labour or Communist party. Offer your services for canvassing, raising funds or a similar activity. This is usually quite a social scene and offers many opportunities for successful meetings.

Archeological Digs
Anyone can go on these. They attract an academic and outdoor kind of Worldlywise, so the company as well as the fresh air will do you good.

Felicity went on a working holiday to Chartres to excavate Roman remains. She had just finished university and was at a loose end until she started full-time work. Immediately in this industrious, friendly atmosphere she met Francis, a wealthy Worldlywise with a taste for travel and the Arts. Although much of her time was to be spent carrying buckets of mud, she had a lot of fun getting to grips with the local dialect and organising lunch – a savoury spread of French bread, local cheeses and charcuterie finished off with gateaux! Francis' job was to document the progress of the excavation by using his drawing and photographic skills. They passed many a carefree evening together exploring bars and restaurants in the town, discussing life and the universe over a glass or two of wine, and some delectable French cuisine! He has remained a close and longstanding friend.

People of all ages take part, although most range between their teens and their mid-thirties. The more scholarly experts tend to be older. If you go along just to watch an archeological dig you can make a few enquiries at the same time. I find the people there are only too glad to have a chat and enlighten you on what they are up to and what they have discovered. There is usually work to be found washing artefacts, numbering items that have been excavated, helping with the work of physically unearthing the particular area. Food needs to be organised. You can find out about digs through the *British Council of Archeology* who publish a bi-monthly bulletin, beginning in January, which includes details of current digs in the back.

The Legal Profession

By its very nature the legal profession carries a high proportion of intellectuals in its midst, including the Wordlywise variety. Details of how to meet him are set out in Chapter Seven, the Professional Type.

Commanding the Attention of Mr Worldlywise

Discourse

Discourse with the opposite sex is at all times food for a flirtation, and no more so than with Mr Worldlywise. You don't have to command his attention this way, however. A most intellectual girlfriend of mine has a handsome Rastafarian live-in-lover as a gentle backdrop, or balance, to her exhausting range of mental activity. He is on another, arguably higher, spiritual plane from her, but they complement each other wonderfully. She talks, he listens! Nonetheless this is the exception rather than the rule.

You may not want to provoke an affair but you may welcome some stimulating conversation or a sage presence as a mental tonic. Minds are deceptively seductive so don't be surprised if you find that the uplifting tonic takes you further. I came together with my first real boyfriend when I was sixteen years old, wrangling endlessly over arguments for and against the communist ideology. At first I wasn't interested in this scruffy, ideological schoolboy whose most convenient meeting point during the school holidays was Harrods, but he was very persuasive, and as we whiled away the hours I began to think again!

No matter how you come across Mr Worldlywise, he is not difficult to approach or engage in conversation. He is interested in communication and expression. If, however, you do find yourself stuck for something to say, as I did at a party where I knew no one, you can always stimulate discourse until dawn with the question. 'Do you believe in love?!'

THREE

The Foreign Type: Mr Faraway

An Attractive Proposition

The grass is always greener on the other side. The idea of a foreign man may conjure up an exotic vision of dark, flashing eyes and burnished skin, or alternatively the enchanting piercing blue eyes and flaxen hair of Scandinavian men. His fresh, new world may bring to life your romantic dream of moonlight drinks under the palms, or faraway yodelling on some snow capped mountain, or of being dressed in silks and cashmere, and made to feel like a queen.

It may appear that Mr Faraway has the sensitivity to make a woman feel more desirable and appreciated than the average English man. It would be unfair to make the generalisation that English men are incapable of making a woman feel feminine; indeed, I am sure that many men would say that English women don't know how to make a man feel masculine, now there's a key thought! But what I am saying is that a little straightforward flattery and attention, a little fantasy, can go a long way beyond the attitude of boring pragmatism that characterises men's handling of women over here. The sport, pub, and cheap chicken-and-chips style may be beginning to get on your nerves!

Women are frequently seduced by Mr Faraway's apparent wealth, although the impression is often deceptive. Even so, while in England he may have that whisper of freedom about him, that lightness of spirit that comes when one is discovering new places on company expenses!

The English social hierarchy is immaterial to most foreigners. In his own country Mr Faraway knows that he can build you up into who he likes. He can make the check-out girl from a Leeds supermarket with a taste for fashion assume the persona of a designer buyer of Japanese labels from the industrial north of England were she to move to somewhere like Turkey or Kenya! But remember, this works both ways. The business card of your exotic graphic designer from Mauritius may prove nothing more than that he is a janitor at the same address!

Being with Mr Faraway throws into relief a problem common to many societies. With regard to relationships time tends to be taken for granted. Four months of dating may in real terms add up to a disjointed week of getting to know one another. This is a poor and unsatisfactory celebration of romance and love which can even heighten feelings of frustration and loneliness. Mr Faraway often has fewer social commitments in England than at home, which leaves him with more time for you. He may even be lonely, in which case you stand to gain his undivided attention.

Intimate communication with any man is delightful, but with Mr Faraway there is added spice. Time spent with a man keen to discover England, or any new country, is very exciting. As everything is new to him there are innumerable ways to pass the hours. Any language barrier is undoubtedly seductive. The fact that he won't be around for long naturally intensifies the rapport. This in turn means that you will make the most of your time together. To top it all there is the intriguing prospect of visiting him abroad at a later date!

Mr Faraway is good for your sexual repertoire. As long as you take a trip to the chemist before, you can let your passions run their full course with Mr Faraway without the fear of embarrassment or of compromising your reputation. As one well travelled moneybags put it, 'An English girl in Brazil can have all the experience she wants, in several colours. She wouldn't get away with it here!' However, even over here, she might gain a lot more sexual experience with Mr Faraway than she would were she to confine herself to English men.

On the Negative Side

Bear in mind that Mr Faraway may not be with you for long. Before you know it you may find yourself back to square one and deserted. In other words watch out that you don't fall in love, or in lust, and take up courses in Hebrew or Bulgarian, only to be left sending unanswered letters to an attractive swine. He will probably enjoy the flattery and, like an Aborigine returning from 'walkabout', resume life untouched in the foreign tribe from which he came. If you find yourself in a similar predicament then take heart and put it down as a character building experience. Live for the moment!

The worst story I have heard along these lines is of a sweet, homely, Filipino woman who married an Indian man in England. She had his child, who she reluctantly sent to the Philippines to be brought up by her family over there. Meanwhile, she sent them over money, which she earned from cleaning and nursing. After three years she had managed to save enough money to visit her son, as well as to put down the deposit for a mortgage on their home. At the last minute her mother-in-law in India fell sick, so instead she gave her husband all the money she had saved so that he could pay for a flight to India. After six weeks he returned, but not alone. To her horror he arrived on their doorstep with a woman, who was apparently also his wife, and three children. It was a bigamous marriage and neither woman knew of the other's existence. The Filipino woman lost her money and to add insult to injury she ended up having to pay for her divorce.

Life with Mr Faraway in his own country can be very different to what you are used to at home. For example, you've probably never even seen his prayer mat in England, but to your surprise out it comes five times a day in his own home; or against your wishes, you are forced to accept that your son must be circumcised; and you can put away those dashing mini skirts he once found so attractive, along with your way-out wardrobe.

45

The illusion of wealth is likely to fade. You may find yourself alienated abroad, in a country whose language you don't speak, whose customs you abhor and whose religious dogma you are obliged to respect. Now it's convention and modesty which rule the roost! And to top it all, your husband is probably no longer a free agent but a quaking pawn pushed around by the manipulative family finger, one which you most definitely would prefer to have nothing to do with!

Ways of Meeting Foreign Men Abroad

Go on Holiday Alone

You are forced to meet the indigenous population if you travel abroad alone. This is not always the case if you go abroad with a friend. Here are a couple of examples of the sort of meeting I am talking about.

Beatrice was a sophisticated and classically beautiful woman, forty-years-old, with long, shining black hair and fine features. She had been married to the same man since she was eighteen, and was in no uncertain terms unhappy with him, and poor. The couple were even taking in lodgers to make ends meet. Her mother-in-law paid for her to go on a cruise to cheer her up. On the cruise she met a worldly and charming Israeli business man, who had, as it were, a finger in every pie. He was evidently extremely wealthy. She kept in contact with him after the holiday, and after a few months filed for a divorce from her husband. She has spent the last twenty years idyllically happy – and in the lap of luxury – with the Mr Faraway in question. For her, life really did begin at forty!

Christine ended up going for a holiday in Portugal alone because her friend dropped out at the last minute. After a few days she met a Portuguese man in a restaurant with whom she passed the rest of her holidays. After she returned to England they kept in touch and wrote to one another. A few months later she returned to Portugal but, unfortunately, he'd omitted to tell her that he had found another girlfriend in the mean time! Once again she had time to kill on her own. Determined not to get bored, Christine took up windsurfing through which she literally bumped into another man. He was a dark, sultry Portuguese in his early thirties; by trade he was a piano tuner and like her he was environmentally conscious. They, too, kept in regular contact when she returned to England – he wisely chose to phone her on Sundays cheap rate and she phoned him on Wednesdays. She took up Portuguese lessons straight away, although he spoke quite good English, and she has since returned to live with him permanently and contentedly in Portugal. As she says; 'If it doesn't work out I will at least return with another language up my sleeve!'

Voluntary Services Overseas

Offer your skills to earn yourself a couple of years abroad with the **VSO (Voluntary Service Overseas)** or a similar organisation such as the **British Red Cross Society**.

I was surprised to learn that even I could realistically envisage spending an interim period of one or two years in this way. It's a life-changing step to take, however. As one volunteer put it, 'You become totally involved, and people are so appreciative that your life really does take on a new meaning.' The average age of the volunteers is thirty-two, but the majority fall in the age groups of late twenties and forties, that is before they have families or when the children have grown up.

Make sure you pick a country where you find the men attractive! Elaine, a kind and outgoing twenty-five-year-old concert manager, upped and left for China on completion of a one month Teaching English as a Foreign Language (TEFL) course. It was hearing Jane Glover on the television teaching Mozart in Beijing that originally captured her imagination and inspired her to go out to China. Within two months she had met her future husband, a Chinese doctor, who worked in one of the hospitals in which she taught. But he wasn't the only one who was interested in her. An unsophisticated guy in the district came round to win her heart with three hundred eggs and a skinned hare. For the next hour she replaced the eggs in the basket as fast as he took them out!

Kibbutzim

Kibbutzim are *the* place to go abroad to meet foreign men. A kibbutz is a communal society in Israel numbering anything between fifty and a thousand people, where you can either live permanently or where you can go along as a working visitor. It is a cheap option. The quota of hard work required in order to earn your keep on the kibbutz is compensated by the fun of discovering Israel, I think that is the term used. Although you probably won't go further than the beach most of the time! You only need to commit yourself for between one month and a maximum of six. See **Kibbutz** representatives.

Romances come to light in this atmosphere where people of all ages, nationalities, and backgrounds share and experience, as equals, a different culture. From all accounts there is a good deal of partying too. Unfortunately, though, unless you are Jewish, relationships with the strikingly good-looking Jewish boys on the Kibbutz are positively discouraged. Perhaps because there is no bedroom pressure (there are segregated sleeping arrangements) the set up is all the more successful. It must be said that such obstacles don't ever make any odds to the course of true love anyway. It always finds a way around them!

Horses

If you can ride, try working abroad as a groom. Kirsty, a twenty-three-year-old riding instructress, left England for a job in France on the strength of an advert she had seen in the back of *Horse and Hound* magazine. A suave fashion clothes wholesaler called Jacques went for a ride one morning at the stables where she was working. It wasn't long before everything turned in her favour. She is now married to him and in partnership with the woman for whom she went to work originally, quite apart from being the possessor of an enviably chic wardrobe!

Isabelle went out to Italy to learn about race horses. She ended up breaking off her veterinary degree course in England in order to concentrate on her ultimate dream – to build up her own racing stables over there. She has succeeded very well, and is now married to an Italian engineer who she met while perfecting her Italian on a university course in Florence.

Spoken English

Take up an opportunity to give spoken English lessons to Mr Faraway himself, or to his children. It is a good means of earning some extra money if you are already abroad, without involving yourself in too much hard work. Ask around.

Katherine stumbled across her future husband in Spain on account of her best friend's appalling driving! For the second time in ten days the same man, 'Dark, with heavenly green eyes', had helped them out of a ditch. While chatting to them he asked if either of them would like to speak English to his fourteen-year-old son for a few mornings each week. As Katherine was in Spain primarily to learn Spanish, she thought such an opportunity might help her as well, so she decided to give it a go. Indeed, the opportunity was more than helpful. To her surprise she eventually married the owner of those heavenly green eyes! He was a ship's engineer. She had been attracted by his eyes, but only superficially. She had at first found him personable but no more. However, as she gradually got to know him, his kindness and protective nature – qualities that she had never really appreciated before – finally won her over. From what I gathered he ended up giving her more lessons in Spanish than she ever gave his son in English!

If you are on English soil look out for appropriate advertisements in newspapers or magazines with a foreign readership. I knew a woman in her late thirties who took up a position in Switzerland through a newspaper personal column. The job was to speak English to a nine-year-old girl over the summer holidays. She found herself in sumptuous surroundings and in the lap of luxury, together with a delightful gentleman to have dinner with every evening! She is now living on a more permanent basis with the millionaire divorcee father in question!

Au Pair

Au pair work, which you can find out about through **agencies** and for example the weekly *Lady* magazine, is an excellent vehicle for meeting Mr Faraway. As a newcomer, introductions are naturally precipitated in the family circle in which you find yourself. Because you are in a respectable situation you are all the more approachable. Men use the excuse that they want to practise their English on you, but more often than not the truth is that a peaches-and-cream English girl is an exciting prospect, and they just want a reason to get to know her.

I met numerous Italian men while working as an au pair in Venice. Every morning I had to take my spoilt, brown-eyed *bambino* to the beach for three hours. He spent his time fishing for crabs and playing and I either chatted with other au pairs on the beach and made numerous friends through them, or chatted non-stop with as many gorgeous, deeply tanned Italian boys as I liked. I spent most of the time practising my very rough Italian on them, and they were only too delighted to help me.

Many women do end up settling down in the country in which they work – at least for a while. Tina, a twenty-year-old American language student, is a case in point. She worked as an au pair in Berlin and was introduced through the family to her future husband, now of eleven years' standing.

Tracy, in between school and university, took up an au pair job in Finland which entailed looking after six-year-old twin girls and a menagerie of animals during working hours. She went out with a Finn she met over there but had to return to Leeds to take up her course and was naturally heartbroken. On balance she says that the experience was enriching and therefore worthwhile.

Newspaper Ad

'Courier for a rambling expedition in Greece' was an advert in a newspaper which caught Kate's imagination. She had just finished a Master of Arts degree and wanted to go abroad, but didn't have any money. A working holiday like this was the perfect compromise.

It was raining on the island one weekend, so she returned to base with a few of the tour; some of the others were gluttons for punishment and struggled on in spite of the rain. They were given a lift in a Mercedes by George, a lithe Greek, with bleached blond hair. Their intention was to go to a Bazouki club that evening, so he suggested that they went along to his favourite haunt. To cut a long story short, Kate married George later that year. Unfortunately it didn't work out because he was madly possessive and expected her to adopt the role of a servile wife! Nevertheless the story illustrates the point that if you find work abroad you are in a perfect position to foster relationships with appealing Mr Faraways!

Strategy on Home Ground

Waitressing

Waitress work in a non-English restaurant is an excellent opportunity to meet foreign business men, and foreign students in particular. Neither set of people are likely to grace the table of an English restaurant. It just takes friendly waitressing to break the ice, which can in turn lead easily to a rendezvous outside of working hours.

Sue and Betty, a couple of girls who were working in a popular wine bar in London, made the acquaintance of Henri, a French engineer who was passing through before he went off to work on a project in Turkey. They later joined him out there, one for a romance, the other for the ride!

Sarah was holding down a well-paid job as a legal secretary but she decided that she wanted a complete change of scene. To everyone's surprise she took up work in an Italian restaurant on Saturday nights. She continued working there

51

for over a year because she enjoyed the bubbly continental crowd who ate there, and especially the men! Her confidence in the presence of men improved no end, and, to boot, she was paid for it.

Quite apart from the clientele, some of the staff are likely to come from abroad. Not just your Luigi-spaghetti-heads but foreign students like André, a Belgian dramatic arts student. He was studying the London night life – from S & M (sado-masochist) parties, to National Theatre productions. He needed to earn some money and ended up going out with Sonia, a language undergraduate from Birmingham, who worked in the same restaurant as he did over the summer.

Teaching

There are many interesting opportunities to be taken up through teaching English to foreign students. You don't need to speak a foreign language but usually you need to do a language course which you can find out about through the RSA or International House. Women of all ages may be interested in this option because, although naturally there are many young students to each, there are also just as many older business and professional men as well. You can either teach at home or abroad. If you teach in England you will probably run reasonably intensive courses which will put you into contact with around sixteen students a day. You must always remember that if you start amorous relations with one of your foreign students, he may well be returning to his own country in the not too distant future. However, fear of having to say goodbye didn't deter a friend of mine from having a whale of a time teaching English in London one summer. Men of all nationalities never stopped asking her out for drinks and meals. She was showered with gifts at the end of term. If nothing else it did wonders for her ego.

The odds on meeting and drawing closer to a dashing Mr Faraway are heightened if you teach abroad. Firstly, there will be more part-time students, so there will be more choice! Secondly, the courses are likely to be less intensive so you will be seeing him over a longer period of time. Thirdly, language classes are usually small, which means you get to know your students well! I made good friends with some of the students that I taught in Milan. They were hospitable and eager for me to appreciate their country. I found that visiting Como and Stresa by the picturesque mountain lakes north of the city in a car with a bubbly group of Italians was infinitely more enjoyable than coping with trains or on foot with a guide book! In return for their attentions they were able to practise their English on me. This has to be one of the best ways of meeting foreign men.

Another way to obtain a teaching job is to offer your services as a language teacher to an international company which does internal foreign exchanges from time to time. Alternatively, advertise your services on the company noticeboard.

Room to Rent

If you are a home owner you might consider letting a room to a foreign business man or student. You could land yourself with an interesting lodger to brighten up the winter evenings, and if not him, at least one of his friends! One of the best ways to do this is to put yourself on the accommodation list of an English language school. There is one in most big cities. You are able to express a preference for country of origin, sex and age group.

Jill, a tall, auburn thirty-two-year-old bank clerk, recently divorced and short of money, decided to kill two birds with one stone. She contacted the local language school in Bristol and took on a lodger to take the edge off her loneliness as well as give herself another source of income. She soon found herself sharing with a charming Dutch man. This led to her being introduced to, among others, his handsome elder brother, with whom she ended up going on a romantic holiday to Ireland.

Alternatively advertise in a newsagent's window, or in an English or foreign newspaper. Specify the type of Mr Faraway that you want. Perhaps you've always fancied the idea of a South American business man! Another option is to look

53

on the notice boards of colleges with a high foreign student intake. See who is looking for accommodation, or, like this music student did, look for yourself.

Fed up with the 'neurotic, introverted musicians' of her college, twenty-three-year-old Deborah took it upon herself to wander along to the noticeboard of a more affluent college than her own, with a high foreign student intake. Within the month she found herself in a large, shared house with three men and a woman – a bohemian Norwegian artist, a German designer, an Italian architect, and a female Yugoslavian business undergraduate. Although they all lived very independently they obviously ran into one another frequently, especially Deborah and the German designer who hit it off particularly well. The new arrangement put her life in a new perspective and did her confidence the world of good!

During my first year at university I got the chance to run a house off Eaton Square for an Italian business man and his half-Mexican son, who was an old school friend. I had called in on him one day to see how things were going. They were evidently going very well. He proudly showed me around his house and, as luck would have it, told me his father was now looking for a housekeeper. Not one to miss an opportunity, I offered my services. I had to earn my keep, but in return I gained an interesting social life and best of all, one of his good looking Latin friends as a boyfriend. It was just like looking after my own house, only I was neater when 'Papa' was around, but then so was his son. I do realise I was lucky, however I didn't hesitate to take up an opportunity when it presented itself!

International Companies
Look for work in an international company. There are always possibilities to move to fresh pastures if you are footloose and fancy free and your situation is beginning to feel somewhat stale. As an English woman abroad you will attract attention. Be brave! Set off in the positive spirit that you can learn languages, and that Mr Faraway loves women!

54

Helen, a non-French-speaking American executive, had been sent to work in Paris. After three days over there, she was still preoccupied with the waiter who had served her on her first day. For that reason she was now having a sandwich at this same chic café. Unfortunately, it was his day off, so she was glum to say the least and she had no intention of reciprocating the interest shown by the table of guys to the left.

She absentmindedly began to cut her sandwich and in the process caused a good deal of it to spin off in the direction of another table to the right, occupied by a humourless French couple. Utterly embarrassed at having drawn so much attention to herself by her clumsiness, she diverted her eyes to the table of guys on her left to seek reassurance. They were evidently amused by the spectacle and one of them asked, 'Would you like to start your déjeuner again wiz us?' She didn't hesitate to accept their invitation and ended up walking away from the table with one of them who became her first Parisian boyfriend, although ironically he was Dutch!

Don't underestimate the powers of a telephone rapport. Anna, a loquacious twenty-six-year-old, worked as a foreign exchange trader in a Japanese bank in London. She used to be on the phone constantly to Axel, her counterpart in Germany. Evidently he was talented at making money, but he also had serious aspirations in the music business. After about six months of uplifting conversations that were gradually getting longer and longer – two minutes of business and half an hour of flirtatious chat – Axel asked her out to Germany for a weekend. She was apprehensive in case the meeting was a disappointment and the rapport was ruined, especially when he told her to look out for a tall blond guy in pink jeans tucked into cowboy boots, which she didn't think was quite her style! In fact she was met by a fine looking guy, dressed as described, who welcomed her with a warm, open smile. Within minutes they had fallen head over heels in love with each other. The relationship progressed and for the past two years they have been living together in Germany. Axel has since opened a recording studio in which Anna has become involved, developing her own musical talents.

Hotel Work

Hotel receptionist work often brings you directly into contact with Mr Faraway. Most encounters are going to be with single business men. The fact that you are one of the first people he meets, and that you will encounter one another every day for as long as he's there, creates the opportunity to become familiar with one another. It is just a question of taking advantage of the opportunity.

Nineteen-year-old Gale worked in a three-star hotel in Winchester for the summer. For much of the time she was in the reception area, especially as one of the four Americans stationed there with ICI for six months had taken her eye. After a few days some of the staff, including her, were invited to a birthday party given by one of the ICI clients. For once Gale did herself proud. Instead of being shy and withdrawn as she normally was in such a situation, she made a concerted effort to pluck up the courage to make her attraction clear. She placed herself strategically opposite her chosen one and she danced and chatted the night away. Quite sensibly she had convinced herself that she had nothing to lose, after all, one day in the not too distant future he would return to America! By the next day she was back to her normal ways. When she saw him in town she said 'Hullo' and quickly darted off as fast as she could, because she fancied him! As the weeks passed they did manage to establish a relationship, but just as it was getting under way she was transferred to London. It didn't deter him. She had made such an impression that he moved to a London hotel and commuted down to Winchester every day. For the record, they never slept together – a sweet overboard American reaction to an English rose! After two years of very vague contact by the odd postcard, she has recently returned from a very enjoyable three-week holiday with him in the States.

Benefits

Benefits, ie concerts, plays and stalls organised in aid of Third World countries, are usually attended by foreigners. While discussing the merits of a pottery bowl at a market stall, a girlfriend of mine met a Somalian lawyer. She was pleased to accept his invitation to dinner and continues to see him whenever he is in town.

She was fortunate because at that particular time she was not in need of anyone's company. When you are at ease with yourself, or stimulated and in a heightened state of awareness, people are attracted to you like a magnet. This is probably why when you are already going out with someone everyone is chasing you! There is no logical explanation. That's just the way the cookie crumbles. Perhaps you are magnetic because you are free and strong inside. Frustration with life and with oneself has to be one of the greatest obstacles to meeting men! So first and foremost be genuinely interested by the event itself and then, if you have a penchant for foreigners, all the better, but don't go only in order to pick up someone, because you are bound to be disappointed. If you want a one night stand then I am sure your luck will be in – as long as you make it safe!

Delicatessens

Certain delicatessens are a good venue for meeting foreign men indulging themselves in the 'real thing'. Ask him if he knows what such and such a spice or speciality tastes like and with what food it goes best.

Pretty Jeanette, a young supermarket cashier, searching for some decent food in her local delicatessen, asked a foreign-looking man with thick, curly locks where the cardamom was in the shop. He said that he didn't know because he didn't work there. She laughed, embarrassed, and apologised. He continued with a smile, 'No, I come from Yugoslavia, I don't know where anything is . . .' Instead of rushing on about her business, as she would have done normally, she relaxed and asked him what he was doing in

Ipswich. They fell into conversation and ended up chatting in a coffee shop nearby for the next hour and a half.

Foreign Institutes

Foreign Institutes are a perfect meeting ground for Mr Faraway. There is a very high concentration of foreigners here. All manner of activities are organised including films, theatre productions, a study department, and of course a cafeteria. Don't worry if you don't speak a particular institute's language. You can always take up language classes there!

FOUR

The Film And Advertising Type: Mr Shiny

An Attractive Proposition

Mr Shiny has an extrovert personality. He is into everything and anything, and no particular thing. He is game for new ideas and always communicative. He leads a glamorous lifestyle which is supported by a sizeable income. Coming from all walks of life, he is not generally snobby, but he is keen on flashing his money around. Even if this is money which he has to claim back on expenses, it nonetheless makes him an interesting prospect as a passport to glitz.

Don't underestimate the perspicacity of Mr Shiny, for all his apparent superficiality. Although you may like to pigeonhole him there is usually a lot more to him than meets the eye. For a start he probably hasn't always been in advertising, and he probably isn't always going to stay in advertising. A man of experience is always interesting to talk to.

He is exceedingly positive about life. He is bristling with charm. These qualities are often betrayed in a sparkling smile and a permanent twinkle in his eye. Mr Shiny is good with people, ie, he knows how to handle and how to humour them, even if he hates their guts. You don't ever need fear being put on the spot!

To round off this paragon of affability he is streetwise, intelligent, witty and guaranteed to make you smile. All in all he is manipulative, but nice! So what more could you want than a well-rounded character with a luxurious standard of living, who can humour you?

On the Negative Side

Not all men in advertising are wealthy, particularly as advertising has been going through a bit of a rough patch recently, but all of them intend to be. Thus Mr Shiny works within an extremely competitive environment. Those that have made it are very insecure about losing it. Stress, deadlines, budget deficits, ulcers and falling from grace are all pitted against maintaining his jolly veneer.

Some Mr Shinys, in the process of projecting all their enthusiasm and confidence, take on an arrogant, self-opinionated manner. You may find that he is intimidating as opposed to friendly. For his part it is nonetheless an effective manner for 'pulling' attractive women. Women are targets, appendages to flatter Mr Shiny's ego. We are talking power and penis extensions here, Porsches and bimbos. Not all women would want to be a part of such a materialistic and sexist world.

The advertising microcosm manifests itself at its worst in a materialistic man who is bent on instant gratification and prone to everything in excess — drinking, eating, puerile humour, exhibitionism and loving himself to the ends of the earth. In a nutshell, modesty is a word that is not in his vocabulary. For all that, he is a lot of fun and great company.

Mr Shiny's Sort of Woman

Intelligent, confident and sharp, with a hint of spirit for the good times — just like him! A woman of this order will pre-empt any infuriating male chauvinism and bring out the best in Mr Shiny. If you are good looking, all the better. Wealthy women go down a treat as well! Shallow, presentable women, with an eye on all he has to offer, are just as acceptable to him. Generally he seems to feel the need to be noticed in order to enhance his flashy image.

Be Direct

The selling world of Mr Shiny is about seducing the consumer, so don't be afraid of drawing attention to yourself or of being forward. He expects it.

At a media New Year's Eve party, two couples were placed on the same restaurant table. This put a spanner in the works because the respective girl and boyfriend of the different couples took a great liking to one another. At an opportune moment the woman in question — a twenty-nine-year-old agency producer — went to the Ladies thinking, 'Am I going to be very bad? God, he's so nice . . .' As she was doing her hair, Mr Shiny, a six-foot-two good-looking art director, walked in behind her and whispered, 'There is obviously a big attraction. Do you want to do something about it?' They started necking in the Ladies loo and moved across into the Gents where, to keep up the excitement, he proceeded to mouth to her, 'The man who you came in with is in the next door loo . . .' It was a dangerous flirtation but perfectly carried off. By surreptitious footsie footsie and lingering looks all aglow she had made it clear that she fancied him without, I believe, upsetting her partner, although he was, metaphorically speaking, as dead as a dodo at this stage. Mr Shiny had had the balls to take her up on the challenge by going to 'the heart of the matter'!

Don't coyly wait for something to happen. Take the initiative. Remember he's a modern man! On location in Greece, an unsuspecting copywriter in his mid-twenties went to a night club and was asked to dance by a svelte woman who, it emerged, was a Swedish opera singer. She was not a hardened career lady, but someone a bit different. He took to her like a duck to water — for three years! He commented, 'Because much of our relationship was built up through correspondence I got to know her so much better. You have to think a lot about what to write, which stretches you. Her personality in turn came through very strongly in the letters, and she could relate to me. It was great to have an intelligent woman throwing light upon ideas that I was exploring. It is wonderful when someone challenges ideas

63

in your head, to the point where you discover your own feelings. I got to know her so much better than if I was conducting a relationship lazily by the usual dinners and so on.' The language barrier posed them no problems, she even taught him Swedish. Love letters are a good example of the way in which men and women can complement each other psychologically as well as sexually.

Patricia, a twenty-nine-year-old solicitor, approached Ali, a bubbly young Indian man at a party, 'I love your shoes. I was sitting behind you and I noticed your shoes. What do you do in life?' He was an assistant film producer. Immediately he warmed to her. He described her as, 'Chatty, but at the same time she showed her vulnerability. She was a lot older than me and had been going out with someone twice her age, so she had made up her mind to catch someone young again. She was honest, not demure, and knew how to go about meeting someone.' Ali was delighted that she had made herself known to him. They ended up having an intimate and longstanding relationship.

Give as good as you get! Juliette, a cheerful thirty-one-year-old actress, was stood up one Friday night at Zazou's wine bar. Needless to say, she felt a real gooseberry amongst the Shiny buzz. She stepped back from the bar and accidentally knocked the man who was standing behind her. He endeavoured to put her down and embarrass her, 'If you're trying to pick someone up, darling, I shouldn't go into them backwards, I should go into them forwards with tits like that.'

She didn't dissolve into nervous giggles or go into a hot flush, but retorted with a supercilious smile, 'I would never try and pick up a man who dressed with such appalling taste,' and went to sit down.

She was joined by a man who she described as 'the most beautiful man I had ever seen'. He was one of the three other men that the MCP had been with. Suspicious that they were in cahoots, her reply to his line, 'I'd like to know you better', was pretty terse: 'If you want a fuck, forget it.' It turned out that he was genuine and he wasn't put off by her bluntness. He is an American graphic designer and they now live together.

Where to Meet Mr Shiny

Soho Hangouts
In London, Soho is the heart of the film and advertising world. This is where it's at! Media society hang out here in cafés, bars, clubs and restaurants such as Kettners, Zazou's, the Soho Brasserie, Groucho's, Braganza, Fred's, the Pollo restaurant, the French pub in Dean Street, to say nothing of the exclusive, wickedly priced restaurants such as Le Jardin des Gourmets, Le Caprice, Sutherland's and Orso. Here they while away many a smooth-tongued hour with clients, over lunch the length of an afternoon, and sometimes dinner! If you have trouble here, then find the addresses of the various advertising agencies, most of which are in the West End of London, and search out their local pubs. Although the atmosphere can be a little cliquey I don't think it would take much for a couple of pretty women to break the ice! Simply hang around these fashionable media venues, perhaps with a friend for moral support, until you meet him. A friendly barman may be able to point you towards any regular Mr Shiny customers. From then on it is up to you. A good time to approach Mr Shiny is when his glass is full, when he is alone, or when he is with a male friend.

I am particularly attracted to Mr Shiny's open mind. Nothing really surprises him. Present yourself by genuinely expressing your curiosity to meet the man behind the 'puff' of ads, 'after having read this book . . .' for instance! He will be flattered by your interest, added to which he loves women. Providing he has the time, you can almost depend on him taking you in with a smile at first and then turning on the tap of charm to enlighten you on the ins and outs of advertising. To help the conversation along, I advise you to have a few example of ads that you are fond of up your sleeve. Be ready to hit the town afterwards!'

If you can't handle the above approach place yourself strategically in one of these venues, and then use the usual ploys to get his attention! Ask for a menu, an ashtray, the time, if he has got a pen, or perhaps which wine he would suggest or which course he would recommend. Be ready to do this instead of thinking afterwards 'How the hell could I have got to meet him?' If you have the confidence, an effective but little used trick is to send a bottle of champagne – a glass will do if you can't afford the bottle – over to Mr Shiny's table – but be careful that he is not with a client. It's not as brazen a move as it sounds if you honestly want to meet him, as opposed to jump into bed with him! There is always time for that. Firstly get to know him well!

Softball

If you are of a sporty disposition, and are working for an advertising agency over the summer months, softball is the game to take up. It is increasing in popularity. With teams of ten a side, equally balanced between men and women, it makes for an interesting game. It also creates endless opportunities for flirtations with Mr Shiny. Quite apart from introducing you to some of the employees within your own agency who you probably don't already know, it gives you the opportunity to meet employees from other rival agencies.

Film and Photography Courses

● Film and photography courses are an excellent way to meet interesting Artheart Shinys: the quintessence of artyfarty glam and very in! Apart from anything else there is a snug darkroom in which to get to know one another!

Betty, for example, a vivacious New York advertising executive in her late twenties, took up adult education classes on film makers and film making. It entailed watching a lot of films, which were followed by a question and answer session in a dimly lit theatre – all the ingredients for excellent man-to-woman discussion and repartee. Over the weeks a romance developed between her and a handsome graphic designer.

Sandra, a determined young New Zealand woman, had the right idea about how to handle men. She was on the rebound from a drawn out relationship with a man whom she described as 'a suffocating, jealous Spaniard'. She had decided to redirect the frustration that he had caused her by doing something new and exciting. Thus, in order to get into the film industry, she took up a university extension film making course. There were no other women on the course so she felt at ease. As she put it, 'I've never been successful at landing a bloke at a social event where I have had to compete with other more glamorous and calculating females!'

Two men in particular looked interesting on the course. There was Christopher who was ten years older than her, distinguished with grey hair, and there was Jim who was tall, dark and handsome. He wore grubby jeans, leathers, and rode a big bike, a turn-on she tried to ignore! At that time Sandra was sharing a flat with Leila, a female scientist who had just split up with her husband, so she asked her along to the end-of-course party. She regretted doing so because Leila monopolised Jim's attention while Sandra found herself stuck in a crowded room with Christopher who, by now, bored her to tears. Always resourceful in an emergency, she gathered her thoughts and prepared her *coup de grâce*. As she explained later, 'In a situation like this, one has to be ruthless. Friendships count for nothing when you're decided on the man of your dreams!' She went over to her girlfriend, drew her to the side and said, 'I've introduced you to the wrong one. Christopher, who I am with, is really neat and he wants to meet you – you'll have so much in common you just won't believe it!' Never underestimate female cunning, and never be frightened to use it.

To cut a thirteen-year-story short, she went home with Jim that night and intimated to him that she needed a partner for a wedding in South Island the next day. She offered to pay his air fare if he wanted to join her. They haven't been parted since; they have two lovely children and to all intents and purposes they are the perfect match. Now he is her feature film producer and she is his director.

During the making of one of their films in New Zealand they employed an English nanny called Sally to come over and help look after their children. Her involvement in the film world soon led to romance with Timothy, a six-foot-four blond location manager. She is now blissfully settled with him and their two children in tow, in what Sandra describes as, 'The summer palace, on a rocky mountain looking over the whole of Wellington city.'

The Work Place

A tremendously positive, sociable attitude pervades the whole industry which makes it a cinch to meet and go out with people here. The stress is on public relations, parties, on looking relaxed and on socialising. The aim is to keep the respective agency and company profiles high. Naturally there are a good deal of amorous or lustful goings on behind the scenes, as in any glamorous business. The woman producer who chooses a director, more on the strength of her personal rapport with him than on the merits of his mediocre show reel; or the young musician who seduces the lady at the record company in order to turn the tables in his favour are all part of the game.

If you are an extrovert with a bubbly personality you are way in there. Clara, a fun account executive who had started off as a secretary in advertising, had been transferred to the agency in Paris. She was all set up for a blind date with a guy her former colleague in London had strongly suggested she meet. When they arranged their rendezvous she gave this description of herself, 'I have shoulder length brown hair and I will be wearing a hat.'

He turned up to the rendezvous and about six other women fitted the description. He wasn't confused for long. As he told her, 'I knew which one was you immediately. Who else but an advertising woman would wear a hat with pink lace and ostrich feathers. It was outrageous!'

Hints for Finding a Job in and Around Advertising

Getting into advertising is about being in the right place at the right time, and jumping in there. Once you are in there it is up to you what you make of it. You may find that Mr Shiny is not for you, but if you can find the patience and the humour to tolerate the streetwise cockiness and the generally sexist tone of the place, you are probably either sufficiently thickskinned or clever enough to get along.

● *Secretarial*

One of the simplest and most popular routes into advertising is through secretarial work. You could approach personnel departments directly or a specialist agency like **Pathfinders** with a specific area of advertising in mind and with a view to a future career. Persistence, interest and presentation are vital to set you on your way. Go for temping work around Christmas, because you get to go to all the parties!

Being a creative industry, advertising thrives on originality. There is no reason why your CV should not be as original as this young man's. He was trying for a placement as an account executive and sent a CV which folded out with a piece of mock fuse attached to a mini bomb. It read, 'This is going to explode the advertising world!' You could try something else. One young man got his would-be employer's personal assistant to take a package into her boss. Inside the package was a model of a pair of hairy legs and boots with a tag saying, 'I'm standing at your door until you let me in!' How can Mr Shiny resist such humour and originality?

Modelling

Modelling is an obvious option, but I am not necessarily talking about clothes or glamour modelling. You might be able to consider part modelling. Think of your strong points. Perhaps you have lovely straight hands, well shaped feet, or an extraordinary nose? Get in touch with a **model agency** directly for advice.

TV Work

Mothers are able to put their baby, or child, in the limelight for photo or TV work. You can either put your youngster on to a **child agent**'s books or alternatively you can call up a production company directly. They are only too happy to cut out the agent's fee. If your child is chosen, you will pass numerous hours on location, where you will be exposed to the crew, producers and so forth. This is a fantastic ground for really getting to know some interesting men. Your local library should have a copy of a book called *The Knowledge* which gives names and addresses of production companies throughout England.

Nannies and Make-up Artists

You may like to consider either of these professions. Both will lead you into close proximity with Mr Shiny on a film or TV shoot. A famous comic actor, for example, not long ago married his make-up artist! Many hours are spent on location. Although there is a lot of hype and pandering to the director when on set – everyone to attention – the atmosphere is familiar and informal off set. Early starts and a common goal put actors, technicians and crew, who probably don't know each other very well, on equal terms. No doubt the tension of creativity combined with the stress of meeting deadlines, encourages the coming together of true minds and bodies!

Agency Despatch Department

If you are prepared to use your muscles a little, why not try for work in an agency despatch department. Make it clear that you are prepared to do everything the guys do. It is a foot in the door which many young men take before moving up within the agency. In the same vein you could try for the position of 'runner' in a production company, but you may find all the bawling and hollering at you, as well as the heavy work, a bit too much. You'd know more what to expect in a despatch department.

Sandwich Selling!

If you are enterprising look into the possibility of selling sandwiches around the agencies. They were crying out for them at Saatchis when I worked there. A sandwich-o-gram has been suggested!

The Creatives

The creative side, as you probably already know, literally think up ideas for ads. Teams of highly paid and, note, predominantly *male* art directors and copywriters (those who do the pictures and those who write the words, respectively), hold the floor in many an agency with their imaginative buffoonery and exhibitionism. It is essential that they maintain their 'streetcred' profile in order to catch the imagination of the person on the street. There is less LSD and dope used to oil their minds than in the sixties, but there is still all the craziness. For instance one 'cool' copywriter I know of was married within six months to a particular girl for a £10 bet. I have known of creative teams to play with train sets until five am at the office!

How to Meet the Creatives

● If you are already in the industry, familiarise yourself with the account that your department is dealing with. Alternatively, interest yourself in the briefs that the creatives are wracking their brains with. They are always willing to hear new ideas.

An agency account was looking for new ideas for a brief. Interested in the challenge, together with imaginative Max who worked in the production department, I spent some serious, crazy summer afternoons in the park, over the weekends, and into the early mornings, throwing ideas around with him. Eventually we came up with an idea which we thought would save the agency from losing their precious account and presented it to a couple of creatives. It wasn't in fact us who saved the day, but our endeavours were more than appreciated. We were often asked over for drinks by the

71

creative team in question. I didn't consciously tackle the brief in order to infiltrate the creative department, but on reflection my efforts proved a perfect introduction to it. I might well have had no other reason ever to come into contact with the department.

● If you are temping in an agency you are in a position to present yourself in the creative department on a number of pretexts. You could simply show interest in what the creatives do and how they work. You could make enquiries about taking up a career in this field or ask advice on how to get involved in it. Ask if you could take up any temp positions if someone goes on holiday. They are a relaxed and enthusiastic crowd. Keep badgering them. They know what it's like. Most of them have been through literally hundreds of refusals down the line. And they did not give up!

● **Design and Art Direction** courses are popular with existing teams who want to learn new tricks from old hands. They are equally useful for potential copywriters and art directors who want to learn about the creative side of advertising. It is advisable to team up with a partner so put your name on an agency or art college noticeboard requesting either a potential copywriter or art director to apply with. It shouldn't take long before you find some suitable Mr Shiny. By the nature of what you are doing you have to get on with each other. As a highly successful art director put it 'The relationship between a copywriter and an art director is like a marriage between two artists . . .'

While working at Saatchis I applied to go on such a course at the same time as a video editor whose imagination could no longer be contained within the limitations of his own department. He subsequently became a close friend of mine. We put our heads together, argued over the brief, which you are given in order to qualify, and thereby spent a lot of time together. I didn't get on the course (he did!) but I also realised that I didn't want to devote my life to copywriting. Nonetheless, the attempt was fun, and it gave me a greater appreciation of a creative's work. It thus drew me closer to them.

You don't have to be in the industry to apply to go on these courses. They cost either £50 or £125, depending on whether you are unemployed or not, and take place one evening a week in different London agencies over a period of six weeks. As it is an evening course there is time to go out for a drink afterwards!

FIVE

The Sporty Type: Mr Plimsolls

Mr Plimsolls is the professional, or highly active amateur, sportsman, not the man who watches it on his sitting room television or who merely dabbles in it from time to time, inspired by an expanding belly! He is obsessive about his sport so you had better cultivate some interest in it yourself! I have concentrated on a few of the more glamorous sports. However, the principles involved in meeting Mr Plimsolls should be applicable to any other sport that takes your fancy – if you want to meet a man with a passion for table tennis for example!

For and Against Mr Plimsolls

An achiever of any kind is an exciting prospect. On the other hand, beware that the price Mr Plimsolls pays for his success is singleminded dedication. This means that contrary to all appearances of jovial socialising, he probably doesn't drink, depending on the sport, and on most nights goes to bed early. He has few friends outside his sport and takes hardly any holidays, to say nothing of his rigid routine. The schedule could be along the following lines, as one boxer's ex-wife sarcastically described: 'We'll make love at six pm this evening because I am going to the gym at six forty-five for an hour. After that, at eight, I've arranged a meeting with my coach to discuss the match on Saturday. I should be back around nine thirty and I must go to bed without eating as I am three ounces overweight at the moment.'

One of Mr Plimsolls' greatest attractions is a lean, fit body. If you combine this with his talent and strength of commitment it creates a charismatic ensemble, glittering with travel, excitement and glamour. When he wins, life is rich and fun, fun, fun . . . Mr Plimsolls' two greatest fears are firstly injury, and secondly what he will do with himself when he is past his prime.

The reflected glory associated with a successful Mr Plimsolls is heady stuff but it doesn't really get you anywhere. You will probably be third on his list of priorities, which isn't a great position to be in anyway, after himself and his sport; he probably won't find much time for you. Roseanne, a Cambridge undergraduate studying languages, went out with a swimming champion from another faculty. Inevitably he spent all his time at the pool so she hardly ever saw him. She decided to take up swimming herself. 'If you can't beat him, join him,' she thought. As a swimmer she excelled, but sadly she realised that she wasn't getting any nearer to him because all he was interested in was his own performance!

Despite Mr Plimsolls' many drawbacks women will pay the price to be near him. It is exciting to be close to victory. The associated glamour and glory are an overwhelming attraction. It's a challenge to hold the attention of a man who has such strength of commitment, quite apart from the fact that it's a pleasure to be in the arms of a muscular man with a fit body!

Tips for Meeting Mr Plimsolls

Firstly – Keep Fit

Most Mr Plimsolls are body conscious to a high degree. So take up a sport or get fit. Cultivate healthy eating habits, too. Vigour and vitality are doubly fostered by a competitive nature, but that you either have, or you haven't. In other words, reactivate your body in order to identify with him more easily. It should shake off the desire to binge, tone the mind, enhance the figure and improve confidence, like clockwork. Trim, healthy bodies are attractive to any man, but especially to Mr Plimsolls. It is no use lecturing you on self-discipline and determination because we all know what we *should* do, so all I will say is that you are lucky if you are one of the ones who persevere!

Mr Plimsolls in the Office

Sport transcends social barriers. An office Plimsolls who plays squash, for example, may be asked for a game by anyone from the managing director to the tea lady. Introduce yourself by asking for advice or tuition from a 'hot shot'. Even if you don't play together it will give you something to talk about. Fiona, a quiet woman in her twenties who worked in a travel agency, was bored with life. She thus took up tennis 'for a laugh'. A few months later she met a charming thirty-year-old man in the pub at lunchtime, who worked just over the road from her. They chatted animatedly about her interest in tennis, with which she was persevering, and about his enthusiasm for and achievements in the game. She took a shine to him but he was indifferent to her. Nonetheless, she managed to persuade him to give her some coaching. She called him up at the weekend to keep him to his word. It took no more than a few games to melt the ice on his part!

Join a Club

Join a club and interest yourself in a sport whether at a national or a local level. The idea is a little clichéd perhaps but at least it focuses your energy. The whole palaver generates enthusiasm – many will go just for the novelty value – things happen. While simply making my way towards the athletics club office in Battersea Park, to enquire into the price of joining and opening times, I was approached by a magnificently built man who had been standing by the track. 'When do you come to train next?' he asked!

Better still if you can be like young Nicola and work in a sports club. Nicola worked in a tennis club for six months after she left school, and secured herself a highly sought after British Racquets champion boyfriend who used to practise there.

Helen, a rather serious twenty-two-year-old librarian, on

77

moving from a Devon village to Exeter, brightened up her social life by joining the local running club. She met Steve, a twenty-eight-year-old university lecturer in classic French poetry whilst out training one day. Now they enter marathons together all over the country.

Enquiry into any game provides endless scope for conversation with Mr Plimsolls, especially if you go to something terribly male-orientated like pistol-shooting, archery or karate. He is always dying both to enlighten you and to demonstrate to you his manly prowess! Go on, help yourself. You don't have to fancy him to satisfy your curiosity!

Sports Shopping

If you are feeling bright-eyed and bushy-tailed, and perhaps a little daring, go 'sports shopping'. Approach Mr Plimsolls while he is browsing in a sports shop or the sports department of a big department store. Ask relevant questions about the sport associated with the clothes or equipment that he is looking at, depending on the kind of sportsman you would like to meet. This goes for magazine and bookshops too. If you see him taking down a book on golf, or a magazine on show jumping, then the chances are that he has an interest in the subject which you may be able to pick him up on. You obviously have to be genuinely curious to carry this off, but if you have made up your mind that you want to let a breath of fresh air into your life, then you surely will be.

Glamour Sports

Motor Racing

Power, proficiency and glory converge here. Macho imagery abounds! To endorse this image the men involved in motor racing tend to go for the archetypal model, dancegirl, actress woman! The age range of Grand Prix racing drivers is approximately nineteen to thirty-five. Fifteen to twenty per cent of them are married but it has to be said that from all accounts this minority tend to have 'bits on the side'!

Where to meet the motor racing crowd: at work

It is surprisingly easy for a woman to become involved in the glamorous motor racing world. Here are some ideas on how.

- The competitors' area.   Enquire after work in one of the Hospitality Units in the competitors' area where they sell drinks and light refreshments. Only drivers and teams are allowed here, so you stand a very good chance of interesting encounters. The work is sporadic and therefore suits those who do not have the time or the inclination to involve themselves in a full-time career. These specialist supply companies are advertised in the *Motor Sport Directory* or in numerous car magazines.
- Circuit marshalls.   All motor racing circuits need circuit marshalls who are recruited through the **Marshalls Club**. Their main job is to stand at the side of the tracks and signal the drivers. An eye-catching girl would be just the job! The work is unpaid but it gives you access to the pits and you are as close to the action as you can be!
- Personal assistant.   A secretary or personal assistant should make the most of her position in the motor racing industry. Men in motor racing are usually preoccupied with their machines and under far too much pressure to give enough time to entertaining clients. She is thus quite likely to be playing a key role in public relations – often with overseas customers.

You might be lucky like Brigitte, a single mother who took up a job advertised in a car magazine. The job was to accompany and assist the managing director of a racing car firm during the racing season, on his flights by light aircraft in between circuits. She had the time of her life accompanying him on trips from Monte Carlo to Silverstone and across to Nuremburg. Although she had no qualifications and didn't excel at the job, she overcame those obstacles because she is now married to this same man!

Job vacancies are usually advertised in motor magazines such as *Autosport* or *Motoring News*. Alternatively put your own ad in one of these magazines or go along to a motor race and ask around. It's a great ploy for meeting Mr Plimsolls!

In Action

● On the circuit.   Obtain a racing calendar from the organisers of the various circuits or from a car magazine. The season is from March until October. Go along, and at the gate buy yourself firstly a normal ticket and then a paddock pass. Although the pass doesn't allow you down into the pits you won't miss much – you can't hear anything because of the din of roaring engines, and no-one wants to speak to you anyway. It lets you into the stands and around to where the cars are being primed before and after the race.

Naturally the team, ie designers, mechanics, drivers and sponsors, are around, as well as aspiring drivers. Familiarising yourself with the profusion of men shouldn't be a problem, although I suggest that you have a look at some basic terms associated with cars so as not to be caught out in shameful ignorance. And don't for example express amazement when you see that the tyres on a racing car have no tread on them. Only wet weather tyres ever have tread on them in motor racing.

There is a lot of fun to be had through this kind of socialising, which will stand you in good stead for any future relations you may wish to have with the motor racing world.

● Popular lines of introduction.   'How has the season gone?', 'How do you hope to do?' or 'How did you do?', 'Are there any women drivers in your team?', 'Where are you racing next?', 'Will you be with the same team next year?' and so on. Motor racing is all that will be on his mind! If you really want to impress him and provoke conversation, ask something technical like how many horse power or how many cylinders his engine has!

● Stop watch.   One way to make yourself indispensable is to take a stop watch with you to practices. This is exactly how Judy, a petite Malaysian woman who looks quite incongruous amongst the turmoil and agitated frenzy of motor racing, met a formula three driver who she fancied and later married in Australia. She introduced herself sweetly and simply, 'Would you like some help with recording lap times?' Like many motor racing girlfriends and wives, she continues to help in this way.

● Racing car show. The Racing Car Show at Olympia in mid-January is, of course, a haven for motor racing people from all over the world. Never be afraid to start talking to him here. You will find this cosmopolitan man easy to approach. By nature he's enthusiastic, and he is bound to be encouraged by your interest and only too glad to give you tips on where to go, how to go about it, etc.

If you think you would feel a little self-conscious amongst all these enthusiasts, maybe this anecdote will encourage you – and not just in this situation. Two girls and two guys were at a motor show in America. They were sitting on a terrace having drinks. One of them, Cleo, who was a secretary in the media, caught the eye of a man in his mid-twenties who had been looking at her. He took her fancy but she didn't have a pretext on which to talk to him. It was impossible to approach him with all of his mates around and she knew that he wouldn't come over to her. It looked as though she was with a boyfriend. As the chances of her ever seeing him again were so slim she took the risk of writing a note, 'If you are still interested tomorrow, call me on this number . . .' She walked up, placed it in his hand and said, 'You might be interested in this.' Naturally it did wonders for his ego but more to the point she precipitated quite an affair with a young engine designer, an affair which she would never have had if she hadn't played with fate a little!

● Learn to fly. If you have enough money and fancy the idea of getting yourself airborn, why not learn to fly? If you then fly to the various aerodromes nearest to the race meetings, you are bound to bump into him! Karina, a wealthy highly spirited American lady, made herself known in no uncertain terms to an engineer whose plane, when taxiing from the runway, caught in the wind and tipped the wings of her plane. Understandably irate, she rushed out swearing.

He apologised profusely. They made up and did a lot more than just fly together after that – another little story of how boy meets girl!

● Other associated motor sports.   Car rallies, scrambling, and go-karting, are all likely to attract bold and keen Mr Plimsolls. Involvement in any motor-orientated activity attracts men; similar ideas to those outlined above should be followed if you want to meet him. You may even get hooked on the idea yourself and envisage competing in something like the Classic Pirelli Marathon or the Paris-Dakar race. Make sure you get a dashing Mr Plimsolls to accompany you!

The Sport of Kings

The glamorous, dangerous and phenomenally wealthy world of racing turns out at best (or at worst, depending on how you look at it) highly sexed characters, crazy about women and horses! In fact it has to be said that sex and horses are the most popular subject of conversation in these circles! So, for those with similar passions, you'll have the time of your life! The flat-race season is from the end of March until mid-November and the jump season is from mid-August until the end of May.

A common misconception about male jockeys is that they are all pint sized. They are not. Although most apprentices or flat-race jockeys are light, wiry little men with X-ray eyes, jump jockeys are quite different. They are sturdy men of normal stature with a quite mad, kamikaze nature – but then everyone has this in racing. Their careers are usually over by their mid-thirties because their bodies, or perhaps their minds, are no longer able to withstand the prospect of any more breaks. Even if they are very small – look at Willie Shoemaker – they make up for their lack of body weight in the skill, agility and timing necessary for racing. The bounds of their energy are limitless as is their capacity for fun and laughter. Following the Champion Jockeys dinner at the Savoy in London one leading jockey I met there didn't get back for a nap in Newmarket until five thirty. He went on to win six races that afternoon in Scotland! Strict diet, in many cases 'wasting', and a rigorous regimen are vital to their success, as is their public relations ability. They have to sell their talent to trainers and owners. If they are fortunate, when their racing career is finished they may go on to become anything from trainer to pub landlord to racing presenter, like John Francome. If they are not so lucky they may have to take up work as stable lad!

Where to meet Jockeys: at work
● Racing yards. If you can ride, the best way to meet the racing world – jockeys, trainers, owners and so on – is to work in a racing yard as a stable lass. *Horses in Training* by Raceform gives a list of trainers throughout the country. The only qualification is a survival instinct to protect your skin as much as you can against nasty falls and flying hooves. The only essential is courage. If full-time work is not practical in your situation then take up work simply riding out, for which you will be paid by the 'lot', ie, each ride. You may well be able to do this before you go off to work. A TV producer friend of mine rides out every morning in Buckinghamshire before she goes to Soho to buckle down for the day.

Jockeys either ride out with you every day or they turn up only for the gallops, which are twice a week. An on tap subject of conversation is the horses' performance on the gallops. When he returns your horse to you ask, 'How did she run?' Or ask him advice on how to control your horse, he'll be flattered and you'll be relieved if his advice is effective! As a girl you usually capture their full attention anyway.

Corrine, a pretty, twenty-year-old Parisian student, turned up in Deauville in time to work during the glamorous August meeting. One day she simply returned a '*Bonjour*' to one of the new jockeys who was riding towards her in another string of horses. She came across him in the canteen at lunch and on the nightclub circuit in the evening. She is now happily married to the eligible jockey in question.

83

• On the gallops. In the early morning, particularly on days when they 'work' the horses hard – usually Tuesday and Saturday – jockeys can be found in coffee bars grabbing a bite to eat with the other lads from the yard. The most straightforward line of introduction is to ask him to direct you to the gallops, or to ask if he has any tips for the week ahead. He never does, but it is worthwhile asking! Perhaps ask him which yard he is attached to, when he is racing next. Doubtless he will suggest you go along. When you do go along wish him good luck, or search him out after the race and offer to buy him a drink.

• Personal assistant. If you would like to be involved in the racing world but you aren't foolhardy enough to ride the mettlesome beasts, look out for a position as personal assistant in a racing stables. Apart from the fact that you will be safer, you will be dealing with the Mr Moneybags owners. That in itself is an appealing prospect! You will also be in close contact with the jockeys, arranging fixtures, rides, pay and so on.

• St John's ambulance. Work as a St John's Ambulance volunteer. In this position jockeys will just fall at your feet! If you see at the races, or hear that a jockey has been hospitalised, pay him a visit. For that matter anyone can pay a jockey a visit in hospital. Introduce yourself along the lines of, 'I saw you fall the other day and as I was passing this way I thought I'd come in and see how you are feeling . . .' It will do wonders for his morale and he won't forget you!

• Nurse. Any nurses who fancy the idea of finding out what makes a jockey tick are sure to meet him if they look out for work in a hospital near to any race meetings or training centres. A nurse I met in hospital in the racing town of Chantilly met her jockey husband whilst nursing him there after a fall. I imagine that nurses must have a field day in Liverpool!

• On the track. Retrieve a stick, silk, or whatever item that has fallen during the race, and return it to the weighing room. Whoever it belongs to is likely to be very grateful for its return, and as I have inferred, he really takes little encouragement to pursue flirtations.

• Bloodstock sales (thoroughbred horse sales). You should never be stuck for a topic of conversation here if you know the back end of a horse from the front! There is a lot of discussion on the sort of price that each horse will fetch, and on the merits and faults of each one. The end of the flat-race season marks the beginning of the bloodstock sales in, amongst other places, Ascot, Doncaster, Kentucky and at Tattersalls in Newmarket. Such venues attract an exciting cross section of people. There is every kind of racing character — from breeders to jockeys, lads, trainers, owners — so you can pick up a mine of information, if not friends, along the way.

• Deauville. The bloodstock sales, the race meeting and the High Goal polo tournament all take place in the month of August in Deauville. I defy any English girl not to have the time of her life here whether on holiday or working. There is a beautiful sandy beach on which to pass the afternoons. There are discos, restaurants and casinos in which to pass the evenings, as well as an American film festival. It could be a young — up to thirtyish — or very rich girl's dream! In order to find work you simply have to walk into a stables and ask to see the trainer or head lad. It would be favourable to have a few lines of French up your sleeve but many speak English. Simply ask, 'Do you have any stable–lad work available?' or 'Je cherche du travail. Est-ce que vous auriez du travail comme "lad" chez-vous?' They love the English accent so make the most of it! You are sure to meet jockeys here to say nothing of lads and trainers, and possibly some very wealthy owners too.

At Leisure.
• Many jockeys live fast lives, quite beyond their means. With a few exceptions they are drawn to the good life, and they do everything to keep up the appearance of success. In the evening they can be found in discos, pubs and restaurants near to training grounds. Just ask anyone in a racing town, like Lambourne or Newmarket, where they hang out.

During the summer a two to three week holiday in the

85

Caribbean is arranged for jump jockeys. You can't fail to meet interesting men amongst this crowd of strapping Mr Plimsolls. From what I've heard it is a lot of fun and there is plenty of room for women to join the partying and hilarity. Contact **Sun Living** and apply early on as numbers are limited.

Polo

Polo is an extravagant sport which is soaring in popularity, particularly amongst the 'Moneybags' nestling in London and the south of England. The pleasure and prestige associated with polo, which was originally reserved for princes, lords and dashing guards officers, has now spread to the likes of pop music millionaires, travel promoters, property developers and, of course, the professionals, who earn vast sums of money.

Polo players are reputed to be rich and to womanise! Horses have an uncanny effect on the libido, and polo players, as with the Mr Plimsolls of show jumping and racing, are notorious for their affairs! Because polo is such an expensive sport, the game is frequently taken up later in life, rather than earlier. Players are therefore of mixed ages. On the one hand polo is an excellent means for women to meet fit, charming and interesting men. On the other it is important to realise that polo is a way of life for both professionals and amateurs. If you get involved with a polo man you may end up a polo widow!

Where to Meet Polo Players
● Polo clubs.   Polo is essentially Sociable (with a capital *S*). It is played through a number of associated clubs of differing character from the end of April to mid-September. Most of the socialising is done through introductions — friends of friends on pitches such as Cowdray Park. In Windsor the scene is a little more impersonal — a very chic catwalk for women of all ages. Send a sae to **Cowdray Park Polo Club** in Sussex or the **Guards Polo Club** in Windsor for a fixtures list for the season.

- Polo matches.   Go along to a polo match. At the weekends you usually have to pay in the region of a tenner for
a car, but you can just walk up for nothing if you are on
foot. There will be numerous groups of polo players, not
necessarily playing that day, in the stands and bar area. They
would be only too glad for you to use a bit of feline cunning
to bring about an introduction.

If you go to a tournament such as the Queens or Cartier
run by the Guards Polo Club, and you are put off by the
expensive entry fees – around $18 for the stands – there is
a way around it. Go along to watch the match from the other
side of the pitch to the stands, and then when 'treading in'
starts at half-time ie, treading on the holes in the turf made
by the horses, tread on over into the stands!

The players will be with the ponies near the pitch. I
suggest that you approach and congratulate one of the players
in the winning team there towards the end of the day! Even if
you don't get a chance to speak to him properly that day, at
least you improve your chances for the future.

Another way to meet polo players is to sell equipment on
the riding equipment stands at polo matches. Over a time
you will become familiar with the players. There will be a
permanent pretext for him to return to talk to you – namely
to buy some polo paraphernalia from you!

- Groom.   A straightforward way to mix with polo players
is to become a groom. Advertise your services for the summer
or, better still, go round the polo yards in spring and ask for
work. It's a great way of introducing yourself to the polo
scene, as well as hopefully, finding a job. If you are not
successful the first time your efforts will not be in vain
because the chances are he will remember you if you see
him later on during the season.

- Polo bars and taverns.   Frequent the polo bars and taverns near polo pitches. The players will have few qualms
about approaching you here, or indeed about you approaching them. Like most other sportsmen they love the audience
of women – fun, vivacious and, perhaps, glamorous, 'appendages' – to boost their egos. It encourages their popular

self-image on their horses as 'big, strong cowboys,' and makes them feel good!

● Riding ability.   In order to play polo yourself, firstly you obviously need to be able to ride. Secondly you need to be especially determined because they don't encourage women in the sport. In other words they prefer to play as boys together, and to keep the girls on the ground! However, were you to offer, your riding abilities could come in useful for exercising the ponies. Depending on your fitness, they are not generally too difficult to handle.

● Polo magazines.   Advertise your desire to meet a polo player in the back of one of the polo magazines, 'Likely lass for eligible polo player . . .' It would be just as well to cast your eye over the personal sections yourself to see if there are any ads that you could reply to. It being a specialist magazine, you may well come up trumps.

Golf

Golf pays out high premiums in prize money. It is a sociable and increasingly popular sport. A game lasts about four hours and the season in England is from February until November.

Where to Meet Golfers

● Tournaments.   Go along to a tournament. Simply contact the **Professional Golfing Association** for details. Sophie, who worked in the Nottingham suburbs as a computer trainer, went out of sheer boredom to a golfing tournament with an old school mate. She paid the requisite £2.50 and hasn't looked back since, having created a completely new circle of professional golfing friends. As she puts it, 'It gets you out into the fresh air, which is wonderful if you've been in the office all week. There is the opportunity to pass the time of day with new people, to walk around at leisure and start conversations without any pretext.' In the process of interesting herself in golf, which also gives her the chance to dress up and make the most of herself, she has met and accompanied a professional golfer to a tournament in Portugal. Her new-found glamorous social life has brought her down to work in London, a place she had never contemplated moving to before.

- Golf lessons.   Arrange for golf lessons. They cost approximately £12 an hour. You will then have an appreciation of the skill and accuracy necessary to putt the shots, to earn the sponsorship, to win the game. Then you will be able to pass endless hours discussing their sole topic of conversation along with the weather!

- Pre-match practices.   Watch the golfers practising on the pitch a few days before their match. They are relaxed then and as there are fewer people on these days you are more likely to catch their attention. On the second day of practice, Penny, a twenty-five-year-old technical illustrator, walked around the course and risked a 'Good morning' to a handsome young player who she had watched the day before.

He replied much to her delight, 'Oh, so you're talking to me today . . .' and invited her into the players' lounge for a chat over breakfast. Thus she began her first golfing love affair with a Swedish professional.

- Seafood and champagne tent.   If all else fails, fellow spectators may prove interesting company. In between holes you can always sneak off to the Seafood and Champagne tent in the tented village area, or to the bar for a drink. You don't need to worry about what to talk about to break the ice with all that golf going on around you!

Sea and Water Sports

You will find details of how to meet men here in Chapter One, the Outdoor Type.

Team Sports

I am afraid that the most effective way of meeting men who play in team sports such as rugby and football is to go repeatedly to watch them play! This includes in the early morning or on a dank, dismal winter afternoon! One of the team is bound to ask you along for breakfast, or for a drink if it's in the afternoon. Team members appreciate female encouragement. Besides, it gives them the chance to show off, although they would never admit this! Before long you could even turn into a team mascot!

Congratulate them on their playing. You could ask for an autograph but I don't particularly advocate this to over-eighteen-year-olds, unless it is on behalf of a child! Offer your services as driver of the team coach at the weekends or help to serve the refreshments. Visit any Mr Plimsolls who you hear is in hospital with an injury. He will need all the support and attention he can get.

I don't recommend socialising in the pub with the players after a match. After about twenty Mr Plimsolls have been using some of their most masculine traits all afternoon — aggression and juggernaut strength — it is hardly surprising that the atmosphere is a little boorish and unsavoury for a woman. He is best left alone with his mates to celebrate or console himself.

Cricket

Country cricket is the only all male team sport I can really recommend for meeting Mr Plimsolls. Nonetheless one should always be sensitive to this male enclave of camaraderie. The team of eleven usually represent a cross-section of age and class so there will be a fair choice of individual. The men look good in their whites, the game is leisurely and, best of all, there are always nine players off the pitch at any one time. It lends itself to easy conversations and meetings, especially as men seem to feel at home playing cricket and are usually in a good mood!

One of the greatest purposes of cricket is as a vehicle for aimless, relaxing chatter, for talking about butterflies and bowling. You don't, therefore, need any pretext to go along to a match other than to while away time with a friend or to read a book of an afternoon. Socialising needn't only take place at lunch or teatime. You have all day in which to mingle with the players.

Victoria, a happy-go-lucky sort of woman in the publishing business, went along to a match one afternoon for the first time and watched from the sidelines. One of the players, whom she quite fancied, joined her there for a while. She managed to get hold of his address from one of the other players and, as an unusual, almost surreal, demonstration of her attraction, she sent him a cooked lobster by courier. How could he refuse such an original entreaty to see her again!

An understanding of cricket will impress most cricket minded males. It isn't necessary to be fanatical, just competent on the subject so that you won't have to shut up on cue when they start talking cricket amongst themselves! The best pick up lines of all at a match are, 'Good bowl', 'Well batted', or 'Well fielded.' The object of your admiration won't stop talking to you. Cricket gives men a chance to pat each other on the back and if you, a woman, have noticed his expertise too, well there's nothing stopping you – or him!

After a match the players and spectators usually 'fall out' to the pub together. Despite the friendly atmosphere, don't forget to respect the importance of the cricket lads' time together, like this poor woman did. Joanna, a twenty-six-year-old nursery teacher, who had been dating Russell, a forty-year-old stock broker, for a couple of weeks, decided to spring what she imagined would be a pleasant surprise on him. As he left the cricket pitch one evening she approached him dressed to kill and said, 'Look, I have got two gin and tonics on ice in the car. Why don't we have a drink and then go back to my place for dinner?'

To her amazement he rather stiffly replied, 'That's very kind but I'm busy this evening with the boys.'

Involving yourself in scoring or umpiring would be an extremely popular move. As a restaurateur who spends all his spare time playing cricket put it, 'The first woman I find who can umpire I'll marry!' Preparing or serving teas is another job men hate doing but they will love you for ever if you volunteer. Even if you can only offer one superb tea or lunch every year you will be remembered, and more to the point you stand to meet many an interesting man.

Softball

Softball is by all accounts a perfect way to meet an interesting Mr Plimsolls. It is a summer game which has really taken off in the last few years. The game is similar to rounders and of the ten in any one team, four players must be female. One girl I know took up the game because she used to get so bored of her male friends who played football all afternoon and then retired to the pub to discuss the game all evening. Now she also has fun and discusses the game over a drink at the end of the day with her fellow players. Only she isn't limited to her own sex for company!

You don't need to be fit to play although it is helpful if you were reasonable at sports at school. The age range of players is from late teens to mid-forties. Team members will range from Greek shippers to publishers to advertising people to professionals and pop stars. Although it is quite an affluent set of people who play, absolutely anyone is welcome to participate. The game is governed by the **National Softball Federation**. The season runs from the beginning of April to the beginning of October. It is played usually on weekday evenings and on Sunday afternoons.

Twenty-four-year-old Sacha works in an architect's office and has had the time of her life since she took up the sport a few years ago. She has been out with a jazz musician, an antique restorer and a chartered accountant, and is never stuck for male company. She met one of the above guys through another member of the team who brought him along to watch one afternoon. As in cricket there are nine members of the batting side off the pitch at any one time so it is fun to go along as a spectator too.

Fencing

If you aren't sporty by nature but appreciate a man of grace and agility, then think about this sport. It can be played at any age and is becoming increasingly popular.

Fencing's aristocratic cavalier, romantic, swashbuckling image is carried over from the Renaissance. In England it is usually practised in universities, schools and the Forces. It is a major sport in Italy, France and Germany, where the men proudly sport scars on their faces from duels they have fought. In Hungary, Holland and Belgium it is the national sport. There are thus plenty of opportunities for involvement abroad either as a spectator or, of course, as a participant.

It is a solitary rather than a team sport. Many of those who play used to hate competitive sport at school, but they find that they can express themselves through fencing. Unlike team sports, aggression and competitiveness often work against you in fencing; they detract from self-control. Nonetheless it is energetic in an anaerobic way, which is excellent for the figure. As a sport it is only as strenuous as you make it. It is said to be character building and it improves perception, concentration and co-ordination.

Due to the individualistic nature of the game, it attracts some eccentric characters. A friend of mine gave a humorous description of the wacky members of his fencing club at university, 'It included two Scots, a northern member of a society which recreates civil war battles called the Sealed Knot, a wild Greek, a decidedly romantic Pole, a Jewish Australian millionaire, a six-feet-four pentathlete with a taste for silly hats and dangerous driving, and a very sweet girl who could, and did, drink a pint of spirits without noticeable effect.'

Men and women can compete on an equal footing in fencing. It gives you a chance to beat a man at his own game, which is always good for your confidence! The kind of effect that it had on one six-feet stunt man of about thirteen stone is a case in point. He couldn't handle the fact that his petite eight-stone wife, who trained at the same time as him, was so much better than him, and gave up. More interesting is the chairman of a very big multi-national company who really enjoyed the challenge of having to work hard to beat women at this sport. Only at the top level do men have a significant advantage over women, due to their superior speed and power. You are communicating in one of the purest ways because of the close physical proximity and the high degree of concentration necessary to outwit your opponent. It may be for this reason that so many affairs are initiated through fencing.

Quite apart from a close involvement with one another, the intensity of the game and the beauty of the elegant movements, the costumes for fencing are flattering. There are breast protectors if you're flat chested, masks if you're ugly, and figure-hugging breeches!

There are more than four hundred clubs all over the country. More information can be found by contacting your local Council Office or sports centre. If you are in London contact the old **Amateur Fencing Association**. As it is a major sport on much of the continent there is scope for travel to exchange matches.

Other Contact Sports

Other contact sports such as judo, tai-chi and karate are gaining in popularity. They are also intensely personal and concentrated games which are good for meeting men. The revealing and colourful tunics are quite fetching as well!

Clay Pigeon Shooting

Clay pigeon shooting is one of the fastest growing sports in the country. Although more and more women are going in for it there is still a higher ratio of men to women. There is no need to feel that you will make a fool of yourself because very few men that go in for it can hit anything for quite some time. It is a sport which needs a lot of tuition in the early stages so there is endless scope for a dishy bloke to put his strong arms around you and show you how to shoot. There rarely seems to be enough pretexts for a man to do this, so I would make the most of it and not learn too quickly if I were you!

Any sports shop that sells guns will be able to put you in touch with a clay pigeon club. You can hire a gun, so it is not too expensive a sport.

I have not got the space here to mention every kind of sportsman, but I hope that you will have gathered enough principles from the main sports covered here to enable you to meet any other kind of Mr Plimsolls you fancy, be he motor-cyclist, athlete, show jumper, tennis, rugby or boxing star!

SIX

The Arty Type: Mr Art-heart

Mr Art-heart is an intriguing and attractive character who lives by his particular talent, whether he be an artist, writer, designer, musician, chef, actor or dancer.

For and Against Mr Art-heart

He is an enigma of associations and contradictions:

FOR	AGAINST
extreme highs	extreme lows
understanding	intense
sensitive	vulnerable
passionate	obsessive
kind	selfish
strong	inconsistent
perfectionist	untidy
romantic	idealistic
communicative	loner
exciting	dangerous
extravagant	broke
no routine	unpredictable
freedom lover	tied to his art
temperamental	'cool'
loving	promiscuous
peaceful	radical
big ego	fragile ego!
earnest	flippant

It is no wonder that he needs so much love, space and understanding!

What's in it for You?

There's never a dull moment with Mr Art-heart. No sooner has he finished one project than he changes the focus of his energy to another. It may be working towards a particular concert, play, or performance, writing a book, preparing work for an exhibition or food for a banquet. Unfortunately, such periods of concentrated effort are often associated with unpleasant characteristics. Mr Art-heart is frequently self-centred, self-obsessed and introverted. He lives in an emotional circus of ups and downs. He may sap your own emotional or material resources only to send you ungratefully into the background once he has got his strength back!

Laura, for example, a conductor's wife and mother of two, told me how her husband accused her of being unsupportive of his artistic endeavours, despite the fact that it was she who had paid the mortgage for the past ten years and only she who had ever had a regular income!

There is glory, although it is reflected glory. Association with a successful artist impresses and intrigues people and will put you in the limelight, too. The flip side to the glory is that your social life can become a strain, partly because of his ever-changing anti-social hours. This is especially the case with performers, but it also applies to angst ridden artists and writers. It means that you are often forced, against your wishes, to arrive at partie on your own, albeit to interesting parties! Your social life can become a strain because of the lack of privacy in your personal life or by the fact that there are many untrustworthy sycophants vying for your attention in order to get nearer to him.

There are the fruits of his success to be considered, which may all in all be able to afford you a high standard of living and a good time. If his work is acclaimed sufficiently to take him abroad, you should be able to accompany him on some interesting trips.

Mr Art-heart is renowned for his free, bohemian spirit,

for letting off steam and indulging in hedonistic pleasures such as drink, drugs, sex and rock 'n' roll. Beware of falling in love with this image because the Bacchus pleasure trip can often degenerate into addiction and promiscuity. Such weaknesses may not be the best thing for you in the long term. At the other extreme is the Art-heart recluse whose lifestyle is not obviously appealing. Both types of Art-heart tend to take themselves very seriously and have fragile egos!

He is a romantic and likes beautiful things – why do you think he likes you! The chances are that he is a passionate and sensitive lover. It has been said that a frigid woman will fall in love within three days with a man who has made love to her properly! This could be an explanation for why so many women find him irresistible.

To begin with Mr Art-heart may be obsessive about you. He expresses his feelings through kind gestures, presents, poems, dedication of his time, and so on. In the end, his unreliability, his weaknesses and his selfishness may exasperate you and destroy your image of him as your romantic ideal. But he's not so simple to get away from. When you are at your wits' end he may well win you back with a charming gesture of flowers! All in all, he's exciting, captivating, fun and lovable but you should be wary of his egocentric and complex character.

Suitable Matches

Birds of a Feather
Birds of a feather may find one another irresistible, whether it be a heady romance between leading roles in a play or whether it be two different types of artist! Two Art-hearts in the same field will be sympathetic to each other's way of working, to their vulnerabilities and to their obligations; for instance, two musicians will take it for granted that their social life will seldom synchronise because of their work commitments. There is a sense of camaraderie. They are both in the same boat!

For two artists working in different disciplines, identification and empathy may serve as reassurance and ward off loneliness. The only vulnerability to which this match is susceptible is that ultimately each artist, whether they be a sculptor and a writer, or a singer and a poet, must be egocentric if he or she wants to pursue and truly realise his or her own art. Two egocentric people in the same house can be cold and wearing. Alternatively they can create an atmosphere between them that is highly charged and uncomfortable. Apart from anything else, unless they synchronise their day, they can't depend on one another's attention when they most need it. This can provoke a real arty tantrum! For the most part though, there will be an implicit understanding between birds of a feather which is born out of mutual respect.

Working Together

Working together as a team must make for one of the richest relationships there is, as with Peter and Elizabeth, two professional artists. When I asked Peter if I could speak to his wife in connection with this book he said, 'She won't have anything to say about me, I'm not interesting. But I can tell you, it never ceases to amaze me what an interesting woman I married.' They had met in a library in Edinburgh when they were young and poor. Since then they have built up a reputation together for creating original and highly sought after three-dimensional art, which has taken them all over the world.

The downside in such a relationship is if the common interest created through work (which for them is more often than not pleasure) is removed from them. They may well cease to relate to one another. A cameraman met his actress wife, Linda, on a shoot. She duly gave up her acting career in order to have their children, naturally hoping to be able to keep up some connection with acting through him. Instead, once they were married, he no longer wanted to talk to her about work and she felt more and more cut off from him. Needless to say their marriage failed.

Cultured and Solvent

In the early days, an artist's economic situation is often precarious, so it is as well to be earning a regular income to steady the ship. If you are cultured and solvent you can't go far wrong! You should be able to relate to him and, at the same time, be able to take the edge off the situation when the cards are down and the money is short.

Tamara, a vivacious, cultured, thirty-two-year-old chartered surveyor, is engaged to a forty-year-old writer. He's on the dole and broke, struggling on a £600 advance for a treatise on the works of Shelley. Not a sound investment for her you might say! She's not discouraged because she admires his integrity, has full confidence in his abilities, and has no qualms about supporting him through hard times. She takes the philosophical view of their situation that, 'It almost justifies my inflated salary.' Admittedly she hasn't pitched hook, line and sinker into living with him just yet. She sees him at the weekends, maybe once during the week, and for the most part they live according to his budget, although she sometimes supplements their time together by paying for theatre tickets; she lets him pay for the programmes! He provides the glasses, she supplies the champagne! Their independence gives their relationship an edge. He feels neither responsible for her, nor cramped by her, and she has the freedom and peace of mind that her work affords. This means that when she is with him she can devote herself to him entirely, instead of feeling resentful. They are devoted, without treading on each other's toes.

All Loving, All Giving

The traditional, all-giving female, who wants no more than to feed and look after Mr Art-heart is almost definitely in with a chance with him. If Mr Art-heart goes travelling on the Continent, the charms of a Latin woman who flatters and soothes his ego by giving her doting support sexually, emotionally and if he's lucky, financially, may prove too much to resist. Sadly, the relationship often comes to grief

101

due to boredom once the chase is over. Mr Art-heart appreciates the reassurance of a woman's presence but she must be unobtrusive company. She must not moan about him writing all day or all night, or rehearsing every day and then going away for weeks on tour, or going on an impetuous walkabout, paint brush in hand! Not everyone can handle such a selfless role.

Patty, the middle-aged wife of a jazz musician, who has just taken up teaching infants again now her own children have grown up, philosophically expresses the sentiments of many a musician's wife. 'At the beginning I supported my husband, going along to gigs in the evening. But all too soon I got fed up of sitting in the pub, or club, with a pint in hand, talking to the wives and girlfriends of other musicians in the band. They were nice enough but I wouldn't have chosen their company. If I didn't do that, the alternative was to return after a working day to cook dinner for us both and then to be left with the dirty dishes while he went out to work for the evening! I couldn't handle either choice, so I ended up growing apart from him and developing my own life without him.'

All Others

If you don't fit into any of the above categories, no matter. You only need to be open-minded to be able to meet and relate to Mr Art-heart, to be able to appreciate his company and his art. Fiona, a young graduate working in a book shop, has no knowledge of the film world and yet is going out with a video editor from one of the big London advertising agencies. They get on very well, but to give her some understanding of what he does and to bring herself closer to his social circle, she has admirably taken up a course in video production. An appreciation of each other's activities and interests makes the whole difference to the quality of relationships.

A common obstacle to meeting Mr Art-heart is clearly described by an ex-art student who went to a college where the art school was linked to the engineering school by a corridor. Never the twain would meet. The "art students were dismissed by the students from the engineering school as 'Left wing veggys' and the engineering students were dismissed by the art students as 'Capitalist pigs'". Albeit in a less dramatic way, the same ignorant attitudes persist in the outside world. What a pity. Every woman should, and can, have a Mr Art-heart among her repertoire of friends!

An ideal match for Mr Art-heart is perhaps a woman who has a combination of all the above attributes: understanding, creativity, culture, solvency, patience, independence and most of all the capacity to love him, for all his faults.

Handy Hints for Meeting Mr Art-heart

Move Abode
My advice to you is to install yourself 'where it's at', and to move to an arty area of a town or country as soon as possible. Mr Art-heart is by nature communicative. He is easy to make friends with. Oh, the beauty of not owning your own home!

Sue, a twenty-four-year-old riding instructress, returned to her family home in Leicester to recover from a riding injury. After six months, although she could no longer ride, she was determined to make a fresh start. The town of Bath had long ago captured her imagination so she decided to make a go of it there. She found digs and promptly took up an 'A'level course and some casual work. Within a month she had made friends with some Irish musicians who she had heard playing in a pub. They inspired her to take up the fiddle. She moved to their part of town and launched into it full time, her 'A'level falling by the wayside. In the process of her musical activities she made many new friends, amongst whom were a violinist boyfriend and later a pianist, with whom she is still living!

The following story is along the same lines, although in reverse. Four young Art-heart men, fed up with the grey skies of Ealing, moved to a flat in Camden Town. Their landlord, a quiet bespectacled civil servant, very thoughtfully offered them the company of his daughter Anna, a seventeen-year-old dancer at the Royal Ballet Dance School, 'I've got a young

103

girl who needs someone to take her out at the weekends. She doesn't know anyone around here.' None of them would have dared to ask her out for fear of upsetting him, but how could they resist such an introduction? What a fabulous father! One of them – Sean, a jazz guitarist who works in a fashionable Covent Garden shop during the day – got on with the slender ballerina particularly well and is still seeing her two years later.

Lori, a twenty-seven-year-old career woman, finally moved from her parents' suburban home in Richmond, Surrey to a flat which she had saved up to buy near the arty Portobello Road area in West London. Her social life had been limited by the cost and problems of transport to predictable unexciting evenings out with the same group of friends. She now has a house full of interesting men on tap, and her decisions are spontaneous. For a start she no longer has to plan her weekend! Two days after she had moved into her new flat, she was invited for a welcome drink of tequila by four fun-loving architects who had seen her from their balcony across the road. It may not be so remarkable to be asked over by the neighbours for a drink, but you heighten your chances of meeting an amiable Mr Art-heart by choosing to live in such an arty zone.

Struggling Artists

Apart from a privileged few, all artists have the same Catch-22 situation in common before they are recognised, which is how to keep body and soul together and at the same time develop their artistic career. Some Art-hearts, notably artists and performers, get money from busking, or from demonstrating their talents in the streets or walkways. Musicians may have to play soullessly in hotels, bars or restaurants for bread and butter money. Why not talk to them?

Stock Popular Lines of Introduction

'Where do you play usually? I'd like to come and hear you again', 'Could you give me your number, I'd like to use your talent for a party that I am planning', or, in the case of an unusual instrument like the lute, ask what the instrument is called. You could enquire, as Lucille, an American journalist, did, about its origins. While visiting London, she listened to the dulcet tones of an up and coming lutenist who was playing in a restaurant where she was having dinner with a girlfriend. 'That's a wonderful sound. Where does the instrument come from? What was the piece you were playing? Can I offer you a drink to show my appreciation . . . ?' Thus she befriended him and they went on to spend much of the rest of her time in London together.

Casual Work

Mr Art-heart is often to be found doing menial jobs, most frequently shop or bar work. Michael, a bass opera singer at the Royal Academy of Music, works in a wine shop during the holidays to keep the pennies coming in. Pierre, a Belgian mime student, worked as a waiter during the summer in order to save up for his last year at college. There are those who go even further, like John, an aspiring crime writer who works in an accountant's office, and Antony, another writer, who works in telesales! Or the talented classical guitarist Marco, then in his forties, who used to work as a stable lad in Newmarket. The moral is, don't judge a book by its cover. Make time to have a word with whoever takes your eye. Mr Art-heart will soon reveal his true identity, especially to impress a girl.

Julie, a vibrant advertising character from New York, made a hit this way. She had been enthralled by a swarthy waiter with green eyes and an engaging manner, and saw him again in another bar in Boston two years later. Typically, and commendable of someone in advertising, she didn't hesitate to speak openly to him: 'I remember that laugh. Weren't you the same man who I admired at lunch one day in New York? What are you doing here?' Such a remark is going to flatter anyone, but it is almost guaranteed to sweep an actor off his feet. They talked all night and their friendship developed into a fun relationship. He went on to become a successful movie actor.

Mandy, a hair stylist, successfully hatched an affair with the man she fancied in an Our Price Record shop. She remarked later, 'You could tell from his dress he was arty. He was playing the dishevelled and tough rockstar.' Over a few days she made herself known to him by going into the shop and asking him whether or not he had a particular record. Her *coup de grâce* was when she invited him along to her birthday party, which he was glad to accept. What was a little strange was that there were only two other people there and no presents! The other two left on cue and she was left alone with him. Not surprisingly he didn't mind a bit! Her fun little number had worked a treat.

Arty Party!

Another effective way of meeting Mr Art-heart is for each of say six or seven girlfriends to ask an artist friend, or acquaintance of some sort, along for a dinner party. It would make a most interesting evening. Call it an 'Artists' dinner. It doesn't matter how frail the link, as long as you manage to rustle up some man of an artistic disposition. You may even have to go out and find him!

Take a tip from Sonia, a warm and attractive actress in her early thirties, who temps and does shop work for a basic income. After splitting up from an eleven year relationship Sonia adventurously organised a singles evening along these lines. 'It becomes a strain going to parties when you are over thirty and single because everyone else seems to be paired up. It's not a nice feeling being single amongst a crowd of couples, even if you don't envy them! I have often felt uncomfortably out of place and it does nothing for my confidence. When I was planning for my own party, I knew many women wouldn't turn up for this reason, so I told them beforehand that it was a party with single men only. It was definitely a success, above all for a recently divorced saxophonist and a PR woman who have fallen in love with each other.'

Make an effort and capitalise on opportunities that present themselves. Guy, a twenty-nine-year-old Australian concert pianist, met Belinda, a secretary in a computer software company, at a party and strongly recommended that she read the book, *Bright Lights Big City*. Two days later, to her surprise and delight, she received a copy of the book on her desk at work. Well of course she had to call him up and thank him and she suggested that they go out one night, which they did. They became good friends, and she now finds herself frequently in both his company and the company of his Art-heart friends, 'The time we spend together is relaxing and an interesting change from my usual clique.' The point of the story is that the chances of those two ever meeting again were very slim, because they live in entirely different worlds, but this simple, sensitive move bridged the gap. You don't have to be a man to follow through a recommendation that you have made.

Mr Art-heart Venues

Cultural Venues: Galleries, Museums, Exhibitions
Here there is the time and food for thought. In a relaxed state of mind – you may be admiring a work of art or sitting down and musing over a few of the paintings or exhibits in the room – conversations are easily triggered off. It can work better than a party situation, because you know that you have something in common with those around you, and yet you needn't feel that you *have* to talk to them, that is unless they take your fancy.

Gallery Cafes
Gallery cafés are another excellent haunt for Mr Art-heart. Who knows, you might be lucky. Emily, a tall, sable-headed young woman, was approached in the Tate Gallery café by an equally tall, bashful American, 'with clear soft brown eyes,' who she instantly fell in love with! He sat down at her table and said, 'I hope you don't mind me saying, but I saw you walking around the exhibition and I've fallen love with you.' It transpired that he was studying fine art. Putting yourself into an impersonal setting with people who share your appreciation for the works of well known Art-hearts has got to provoke meetings.

Craft Centres And Bars Close To Colleges Of Art

These are also likely venues for Mr ArtHeart.

Restaurants, Cafés and Bars Close to Theatres

These are usually flavoured with the ambience of Art-hearts. Later on in the evening, after a performance, these places are frequently where the cast or performers end up for a well deserved drink.

Music, Drama or Literature Festivals

Festivals such as the **Bath** or **Glyndebourne** festivals in May, the **Aldeburgh** festival in June, the **Edinburgh International Festival** in August or the **Cheltenham Festival of Literature** in October provide a great opportunity to meet Art-hearts. There is the time to become familiar. If you don't catch the attention of the interesting man in question the first time there is every chance you will be able to meet him in the next couple of days. These sort of events are very sociable, relaxed and exciting occasions that attract Art-hearts and enthusiasts from all over the world.

Borough Council or Regional Arts Associations

Contact the above for information on how to involve yourself in Community Arts. These are projects which aim to encourage art in the community, and may for example involve putting on a play or working in a film co-operative. They can also suggest contacts for voluntary work in galleries, or for stewarding events such as a jazz or world-music gig or even children's entertainment.

Rebecca had moved down from Middlesborough to London for some excitement. She didn't know anyone when she arrived, so it was lonely at first, as London so often is. In between some casual bar work and drawing the dole, she made a concerted effort to involve herself in community arts, and to build up a circle of friends that way. First she did some voluntary work for a gallery. As she said, 'It was especially good being at a first-day opening because there was lots of scope to talk to people. I was particularly excited to meet the artist.' She then went on to join a film co-operative as a prop assistant, and this is where she met her boyfriend of three years' standing, an up and coming script writer!

The Sun

Absorbing the culture, facing challenging situations, new work, new people, new stimulation all lend credibility and reason for the artist to travel, but it must be said that the sun is a great attraction too. Let's face it, not many artists come from, or go to, the North Pole! Thus the continent is a popular place for artists based in cultural centres such as Florence, Paris, Madrid, as well as the smaller Latin towns. Mr Art-heart tends to travel cheaply. If you travel in the same way, you are quite likely to meet him *en route*. Chapter Eight, the Travelling Type, has some useful tips on this subject.

Once you are there, one way to get to grips with the town is to go to craft markets. For instance, in one such market in Albufeira, a town in Portugal, I was chatted up by an elegantly attired jewellery designer who was fluent in four languages and who sold woven bracelets from Brazil for 'summer lovers'. Festivals and galleries are Art-heart meeting points as well, but I have been reliably informed that if you really want to get to the heart of the artworld, you should ask where you can buy dope! You don't have to buy any but the process of finding out where you can is one of the surest ways of breaking into Art-heart circles. Guaranteed!

Foreign Institutes

If you are attracted to a foreign Art-heart but you can't go abroad, do some homework on what is available for you to do at the local foreign institutes. There are endless possibilities here for meetings with cosmopolitan Art-hearts.

Choirs

Numerous relationships are struck up as a result of joining choirs, modern and classical. Polly, in her late thirties, met her husband while singing in a church choral group some ten years ago. She explains, 'He was playing the tuba in the accompanying band and we exchanged amorous glances across the church during the melody. A few weeks later we met in the Post Office and arranged a date.' University choirs are worth bearing in mind as they usually take on non-university members, too. Thus they attract a wide cross section and age range of fresh, new faces.

Art-heart Colleges

Pay the odd visit to an Art-heart college such as the Guildhall or the Bush Davis dance school, or visit the relevant Art-heart faculties at university or polytechnic. The noticeboards in these venues advertise coming events, to which the public are frequently invited. They advertise personal tuition, usually from the students, for whatever art the college specialises in and accommodation too. If you are thinking of moving you might like to share with an Art-heart. Remember that it is enough to get along with someone of either sex, from whichever walk of life you like the sound of, to open up opportunities for meetings with new and interesting men.

Lessons With Mr Art-heart

Why not try your hand at a new art form? Take up the piano or learn to paint in watercolour. An acquaintance of mine called Philippa decided to take up the flute in order to relieve the boredom of the factory line she was working on for the summer. She found a teacher, a Venetian musician called Lorenzo, who advertised in her local music college. The lessons became the highlight of her week in more senses than one. Although she was developing well as a flautist, it emerged after a month that she and Lorenzo were in love with each other. They went out with each other for over a year after which he had to return to work in Italy.

Remember, Mr Art-heart is probably sick to death of the same old faces at college and will be only too delighted to meet someone new himself.

Music Summer Schools

If you can either play a musical instrument or sing to a reasonable standard, music summer schools are a haven for Art-hearts. They attract all ages and walks of life and because of the common interest, friendships are easily forged, as are romances. Carol, a television researcher, and her cellist boyfriend met at one of these schools over the summer. I also heard about an osteopath who met her future husband, a secondary school teacher, this way. Both parties went primarily because of their interest in music, but any common interest shared by men and women creates a favourable atmosphere in which to cultivate long-lasting friendships, or romances.

You can find out about these music summer schools through *Classical Music* magazine. They produce a list of summer schools in two editions, at the beginning of January and middle of February.

Restaurants

The most important member of staff in a restaurant is probably the chef, but you do not often see him. He's a colourful character, never short of a good story to tell. Messages of appreciation for his culinary expertise are sometimes passed on, but he is rarely praised directly. When the rush is off, and the rest of the restaurant are sitting back for a coffee, why not ask to see the chef in order to compliment him personally. Imagine that you have just devoured a succulent *duck à l'orange*, or a mountainous plate of tumbling profiteroles covered in chocolate and oozing with cream, which you have more than appreciated. You would like to invite the chef for a coffee or a brandy! He will be only too glad to get out of the kitchen and meet someone new. He may be accompanied by one of the cooks who is learning the art. If he looks a bit tasty himself, and you would like to get to know him better, tell him, 'That was so good, I'd love you to do that for me at home one day!' He has a routine at odds with the nine-to-fivers, but he gets some days off!

Another way of securing a meeting with a chef is to go to a catering show. These are advertised in the magazine *The*

Caterer' which comes out every Thursday. You could even put an advertisement in here yourself: 'Interesting woman seeks to meet a man about the kitchen!'

British Interior Design Exhibition

The British Interior Design exhibition is an event which attracts a range of interesting men, particularly involved in design and interior design. It is advertised in interior design magazines such as *House & Gardens*. Similar events are advertised in *Art Monthly* and *Artists Newsletter* along with many other Art-Heart activities and diary dates!

Art Fairs

Art fairs, at which the creations of artists and craftsmen are displayed and sold, are a pertinent venue to meet Art-hearts. Keep an eye on the windows of local art shops and the notice board of your local art college for details.

Modelling

No matter what your looks or figure, artists and the drawing studios of art colleges are always looking for people to use as life models for painting, drawing and sculpture, both with and without their clothes on. I have done this, clothed, for some extra cash. After an hour of sitting under a bright light, in an atmosphere of concentration, as though I was no more than an object, I wanted to make sure it was all worth while! In the process of admiring and musing over the class's efforts I met one or two delightful Mr Art-hearts.

Performing Artists

It has to be said that professional artists need the attention of an audience and in their personal life the audience is you!

Jack, a twenty-eight-year-old Scottish opera singer, spoke remorsefully of his brief affair with Helen, a kind and delightful nineteen-year-old Scottish lass, who was the head of one of the John Lewis gardening departments. They met while he was buying a plant for his singing teacher's birthday. She

112

knew nothing, nor it seemed would ever know anything, about opera, and he couldn't get enthused about account balance sheets and organic fertilisers. At least to his credit he tried to; many musicians become quite self-obsessed to the exclusion of all else.

As a general rule an actor's or singer's order of priorities are his role, himself, and then you! Admittedly, Helen was naive and didn't know what she was up against, but total disinterest in his highest priority blunted their future. She would never go to the opera with him because she said that she would be bored, and she would only ever giggle in embarrassment if she heard him practise. A tip for when you meet a performer is to flatter his ego. Give him lots of opportunity to talk about what he is doing and about himself.

Musicians

The first thing to get straight is that you don't need to know a lot about music to show your interest in, or appreciation of, either music or a musician's work. The orchestra are usually to be found in a nearby pub or bar after a concert. It is a perfectly normal and popular move to go along with a friend, of either sex, and to introduce yourself with something along the lines of, 'I went to the concert this evening and I really enjoyed it. I think you deserve a drink, may I treat you . . . ?' or 'Can I trouble you to ask where you will be playing next?' It gives you the chance to meet him again!

Alison, a bright secretary in her early twenties, decided on a whim to go to a concert given by the London Symphony Orchestra. She fell for a violinist on the first desk, and thus went to a number of other concerts in which he was playing. She always made sure to sit in the front row. Front row seats may well prove a good investment, because you get a good look at those who appeal to you! Having caught his eye during the second and third concert, it wasn't difficult to place herself strategically in the bar so that he could come and talk to her. The ensuing affair led to their marriage.

113

Forge an introduction with someone that you admire in the music world, by befriending an associate of theirs. Susie, a vivacious, eighteen-year-old platinum blonde, fell in love with a rockstar in the States. She followed him on tour nearly everywhere. Solely in order to meet him she befriended those who worked around him, including his manager, who ended up falling in love with her. Following her first introduction to the rockstar, he called her name out at the next performance: 'Isn't Susie going to join me up here?' Soon after that she went out with him, and although she had to move to work in England she still sees her rockstar from time to time, whenever he's in London. Six years later he still makes her heart flutter. Unfortunately the manager never did!

Actors

Actors may appear to have a glamorous lifestyle but beware of the superficiality of their world and the fact their most popular subject is themselves and their list of former roles.

Don't hesitate to speak to the actor or actors after a performance. Young actors in particular need and earn their praise. They rely on public opinion for their career development. Ideally they would lock the audience in after a performance and ask them questions. They can't do this, but they would be delighted for you to volunteer your criticism or flattery over a drink afterwards, especially on the first night.

The actors are easy to approach at a fringe performance in a small theatre, as they usually leave ten minutes after the end of a performance out of the audience exit. Apart from this point there is a strong audience involvement, so you are quite likely to have established eye contact with any one of the actors before you meet him.

Questions always get a response! Ask Mr Art-heart why the play was put on, or how long he's been touring. Maybe there is something in your range of knowledge that you can add to his understanding of the play. For instance Melanie, a twenty-six-year-old drama fanatic, on commending one of

114

the main actors in a play about a drag queen, went to dinner with him that evening. She had done a subject in her arts degree in transvestism and transexuality, so she was able to explore the subject further with him. I am speaking figuratively, not literally here!

Don't be coy! Sue, a confident nineteen-year-old arts student, went with a friend to see a popular play in New York. They invested in front stalls tickets. Sue was so taken by the talented lead actor that at the end of the performance she went on her own to congratulate him. In the course of chatting him up she informed him that she would be in England the following month. He mentioned that he would be on tour in London at that time, 'Come and see me again after the show . . .' he suggested. To his delight she did just that and within a year they were married.

Drama societies are a popular way to meet men who are interested in acting. There are endless Amateur Dramatic Societies scattered throughout the country. If you are no good at acting, what about helping with costumes or make-up? You can't get much closer to the actors than that!

Animators

Animators live in a world of fantasy, a world which is inclined to get the better part of them. One elusive animator that I met in the course of my research sleeps in his office and hasn't been on holiday for fourteen years! The pressure of deadlines, together with the time they invest in their own films, means that they work long hours and often over the weekends. But for all that they are some of the most lively and stimulating characters I have met. They have a fresh, child-like quality about them. One I spoke to said that animators observe life avidly as though through the eyes of their childhood. Their inventive humour and boundless energy is enthralling. A flamboyant character started my interview by kissing my hand. He recounted stories of his youth, such as the time he dropped cocaine to a parrot

115

down an air conditioning duct in order to keep it talking all night. He achieved his purpose, which was to annoy the neighbours.

In keeping with the wit of animation, animators specialise in whimsical offbeat or bad-taste jokes. However, like the sad clown, their tomfoolery conceals a vulnerable and sensitive nature. I found this quite disarming as they are working in such a competitive, commercial environment. You can find names and addresses of animation studios in **The Knowledge**, or **The White Book** or the **Creative Handbook**.

Ways To Meet Him
Take note that seventy-five per cent of animators are male and Soho in London is the capital of the animation world. But take note also that Soho is commonly criticised as a 'close knit gossip box', or as being like 'a big school'. All the animators that I spoke to expressed the opinion that they would love to meet some new people, 'It would be like a breath of fresh air.'

● You are most likely to find animators in the Soho pubs, such as the Star & Garter on Poland Street and the Argyll Arms on Argyll Street, either at lunch time or at eightish in the evening. They frequently go there alone to unwind. One of the bar staff will be able to point out any of the animation regulars.

Enquire if it would be possible to have a look around his studios. Approach him with a friend if you are too shy on your own. He will tell you that it is a bit busy at the moment, but perhaps next week. They always say this. Continue to pester him with questions about animation, in the process of which you will get to know him anyway. He is likely to be intrigued, I am sure, by your curiosity.

Lucy, a gregarious young woman who worked in Soho, went on her own to a nearby pub one evening after a hectic day in the office. She chatted to a man who turned out to be an animator. He had to go to a restaurant later on with a client.

As she was going home in the same direction she asked to accompany him to the door of the restaurant in question. On arrival there she asked him if he would like to go out to a football match at the weekend. He was attracted by her spontaneity and welcomed such an original suggestion. The football match was obviously a great success as they are now living together.

- Call a few animation studios and ask to be shown around on the pretext that you are a student who is specialising in animation at art college, or say that you are interested in doing a course in animation but that you would like to know more about it first. Maybe suggest a time at the weekend when the studio is least frenzied. Not everyone will be there, but those who are may well find some time for a bright new woman in their midst!

Ask any of those you meet at the studios about their own animation projects. You may well find someone who is more than willing to show you his fantastic creation, and to gauge your reaction to it. Ask to see the studio showreel – a sort of portfolio on film of the work that the studio has turned out – for another talking point. At the end of your guided tour, you will probably be in a position to ask whoever has shown you around if you could buy him a drink to thank him for his time. See where he takes you, and if he interests you, maybe find yourself there again at a pertinent time. They are a very friendly lot. Call him and ask him to a party, why not? If he can't make it he may suggest another time. If he can, great!

- A direct route into animation is to offer your services for the tracing and painting process of animation in the studio. You will need to do a test for deftness and accuracy judged on the thickness and thinness of line you manage to draw on the clear 'cel' according to their requirements. It is not difficult to do but it can be very skilled. The work attracts many Art-hearts. I know of a textile designer, musician and actress all involved on a freelance basis.

117

Once you are in the business of animation you could cast a spell to get your man, like Annabel. Twenty-five-year-old Annabel was doing 'rendering' work in a studio (the painstaking job of reproducing a picture again and again in order to create the effect of movement necessary for animation sequences) when she met the animator love of her life. More than anything in the world she wanted this man to fall in love with her. In order to allay her frustrations, and in spirit with the animation world, she bought a book of spells. She accordingly stole one of his animation gloves and cast a spell on it at home. In conjunction with the spell she had to both imagine him falling in love with her and she had to will him to fall in love with her. The philosophy is, Get him into your head and get him into your bed! There is a lot to be said for this positive approach. In her case it worked. She is now married to the object of her spell and has a one-year-old baby!

● Mr Art-heart the animator is also to be found at animation festivals. These are held in different venues all around the world – Annecy, Los Angeles, Bristol, London and Zagreb – on a rotating yearly basis. Contact the **British Film Institute** or look in the *Directory of International Film and Video Festivals* in a library for details.

Art Dealers

One of the only Mr Art-hearts whose income you can be assured of is an art dealer, whose interest in the arts is tempered by a shrewd business sense. One art dealer I spoke to described his work as, 'A chance to make money in an amusing way, as well as to meet interesting people.'

Art dealers come from a mixture of backgrounds. Because they need to have had some experience of the art market they don't usually begin to get under way until they are in their thirties. They need to be streetwise and to have presence. Because of all the talk, hype and show that is synonymous with art dealing, it can certainly be labelled a sociable profession.

Where to Meet Him

Antique markets, early in the morning, is the time when all the goods are on offer and dealers do most of their business. Later on the public come. You will also find the professionals at art fairs, auctions and galleries. Don't overlook exhibitions of as yet unknown present day artists, as dealers are always looking for new work to promote.

Talking Points

An art dealer is one of the easiest individuals to fall into conversation with. Far from what you might think, you don't have to have a loud, snooty voice and talk knowledgeably to him about the merits and faults of such and such a painting. You don't have to be intense in order to appreciate a painting either! Simply make enquiries about the prices of objects, pictures and so forth. He is a great one for giving advice as well. Show interest in the piece of work that he is studying as a talking point. Ask him when and where he has next got an exhibition of paintings to sell. Ask him for his opinion on the sort of paintings he would recommend for your house. That way you have the perfect pretext to ask him round!

If you find him behind a stall at an antique market early in the morning or at an art fair, offer to get him a coffee after you have had a chat. He is guaranteed to appreciate such a gesture as it is often difficult for him to leave his stall. If you don't talk for any length of time the first time remember, try and try again. Familiarity may lead to friendship, it doesn't only breed contempt!

Box Office Successes

Concert halls, the theatre, opera and ballet are favourite haunts for any cultured male or Art-heart. Here there are opportunities too good to be missed.

119

This following incident happened by chance but it is simple to contrive. Three tickets had been bought for a five-hour performance of Verdi's *Requiem* but only two of the party were able to turn up. These two, a gay guy and heterosexual girl, decided to try and sell their spare ticket at the door. Sure enough there were a number of people hovering around like vultures after the kill, waiting to pick up leftover tickets. The British norm of queuing is held in abeyance in this situation. People just hang around in a more continental fashion, looking to see from whom they can grab tickets at a reasonable price. These two didn't play the infamous game of touting people at the door, they were even more dastardly and went for the person rather than for the wallet. Running their eyes over the crowd they picked out the most delectable looking man standing alone and asked if he would like to buy their spare ticket. Naturally he did, and given that the tickets were originally bought together, he had to sit down next to them. Their attractive prey insisted on buying them drinks in the interval. At the end of the performance they all went out for a bite to eat together. They exchanged telephone numbers and that was it, the start of a budding friendship between the girl and him. Unfortunately for her friend, he wasn't gay! The 'pick up' turned out to be an affluent builder with a keen taste for opera, a very interesting man by all accounts. So buying one ticket too many and selling it on the door to a man who takes your fancy can prove a very effective way of spending the evening with him!

Another good way of meeting Mr Art-heart is to go on your own to a particularly small and less well known theatre. Footloose and fancy free, who cares what you do? The fact that the performance is a little obscure, or less fashionable, puts you on the same wavelength as all those other discerning characters around you. Remember, men still go to the theatre on their own more often than women do.

A group of English friends, two women and three guys,

120

bought front stall tickets for an avant garde theatre performance in Paris. Right at the back of the sparse audience was a wide-eyed girl sitting on her own, so they asked her if she would like to join them. Albeit a little shyly she did join them, and later they all went on out together for a meal. She continued to see one of them, a fiction writer. The idea of meeting an English gentleman, who turned out to be one of the loves of her life, couldn't have been further from her mind. Having just read the play in question she was simply very interested in seeing it performed in the theatre. The incident once again underlines the point that only when you are utterly at ease with yourself will fate start turning up trumps. You can, of course, do the reverse, go to the theatre in a group and ask a man to join you!

Don't be frightened to treat going to the theatre on your own as a mini adventure, as well as going because you are interested in the entertainment. It doesn't last much more than a couple of hours, nor is it physically dangerous, plus there is a ready subject of conversation should you meet someone there. The bottom line is the more you become involved in life, the more you will have to talk about, and the more you have to talk about the more people you can relate to. This will boost your confidence, and create a snowball effect for encountering interesting men.

Michelle, a slim and chatty career woman in her mid-thirties, had just finished with her boyfriend of three years' standing, a polytechnic law lecturer. Her life was thrown into relief. In other words she had to stand up to herself again, take a good look at what she wanted, and do it as best she could, on her own. She had to do it in spite of her depressed state of mind and loss of self-esteem. 'It was a bit daunting in the beginning but it didn't take long to get back to doing what I wanted,' she said. One of the interests that she had seriously neglected was her passion for opera because of her ex-boyfriend's lack of enthusiasm for it. No comment! She chose to go to Wagner's *Ring Cycle*, an opera played in four parts over four evenings. Because it is difficult for people to organise four consecutive evenings

121

together it is perfectly normal to go to this particular opera on your own. Having recovered from the trauma of her break up, she felt even clearer in her mind about what she wanted from a relationship the next time round. There was no hint of desperation in her thoughts. 'If fate is on my side,' she mused, 'I will sit next to a nice guy this evening.' It was not until the second night, while waiting for the curtain to rise, that her interest was aroused by a rich, resonant voice, 'the tone of Richard Burton', talking to two girls behind her. Taking a breath of fresh air during the interval she found herself standing next to this very man! Not wishing to waste an opportunity she turned to him and said, 'That was a breathtaking first act.' They exchanged a few words and it transpired that he was an English lecturer who was writing a book. That was that until the next evening, when she met him and another couple of people in the queue. On the fourth night the four of them met again and it was suggested that they go back for wine and cheese at his place. After the others had left she continued talking to her host until six am, when he finally walked her to the tube station with, 'Adieu, who knows when the next *Ring Cycle* will be . . . ?' Jolted by this sweet but cold dismissal she panicked inside, 'I've got to say something. I think I've met the man I'm going to marry.' So she said, 'I'm sorry, I thought there was a bit more between us than that.' He said something non-committal and took her telephone number.

It was not until a few days later, by which time she had given up, that she got a call from him to explain that he was sorry he hadn't called earlier but he had been very busy, and would she like to go out for dinner. Her reply was somewhat forward for the ears of a reserved English man, 'I'm too old to play games. Shall I bring my toothbrush?'

Without demurring he answered, 'Yes, that sounds like a good idea.' And thus began a very sound and continuing relationship.

I picked up a couple of tips myself when I ended up on my own at an opera at Covent Garden. My recalcitrant boyfriend was late, so I sat grumpily on my own in the stalls during the interval, waiting. An American gentleman introduced himself, curious to know why I was on my own. I explained to him that I was waiting for a friend. I didn't feel the need to dwell on the fact that the friend in question was my boyfriend of one year standing! I was delighted to talk to someone new. We had plenty of time to establish our mutual interests in the arts and travel. It turned out that he was a conductor and in town for the next week. Not knowing the nature of the friend I was impatiently waiting for, who finally arrived out of breath, he didn't hesitate to ask for my number. I was only too happy to give it. I went out with him several times and he even rang from America and asked me over, all expenses paid, but I called it a day at this point because I was otherwise committed.

So don't waste any opportunity to talk to an interesting man in what is after all a safe situation. Secondly, if you are on your own in the interval, it is a good idea to sit in the stalls rather than to go to the packed bar for a drink. You may well end up being alone in a crowd there.

Direct Approach

Women have often been known to make bold passes at Mr Art-heart. Maybe he is so irresistibly attractive that women can't contain themselves! Maybe women find Mr Art-heart friendly and therefore easy to approach. Undoubtedly much of Mr Art-heart's appeal is to do with his charisma which stems from a belief in himself. Therein, perhaps, lies the answer to meeting interesting men, too. Love *yourself* and they will come running to you! However, even the Art-hearts still complain that we women don't make enough first moves.

Luke, a wayward, six-feet-seven, skinny-as-a-rake artist, who at the time was going through his green and orange dreadlock phase, was nonetheless fondly loved by everyone. Just before he was kicked out from college he went down

123

to Exeter for the weekend and was introduced by a friend to a nineteen-year-old girl working temporarily as a sales assistant. The guy who first introduced them asked her later, 'What would you like for Christmas?'

Without hesitation she replied, 'I'd like Luke tied up in a ribbon and placed on my doorstep.' Luke was appropriately attired and sent around to her house in the snow on Christmas Day. She was so delighted that she just flung her arms around him. They went out together for over a year, but finally he went off alone on his travels to live on a kibbutz. Well, they say all good things have to come to an end.

David, a first-year singer at music college, was an introspective, morose kind of artist. He kept to himself and avoided talking to anyone if he could help it. Occasionally though, contact with fellow musicians was unavoidable. Following his part in an external production, he could not escape a drink at the cast party afterwards. Hidden up in the corner on his own with his drink, one of the robust girls in the production, who was also from his college, sat herself down next to him. She mischievously exclaimed, 'I suppose we're not good enough for you. You don't want to speak to us.' Taken aback by her candour he nervously explained that he thought her crowd were much 'too cool' for boring old him. In so many words he admitted that he was shy and introverted. Nonetheless, from the following day forth at college she continued to badger him, and insisted that he chat with her. Having taken the initiative and disturbed his introspective solitude with her playful confrontation, a long relationship developed between them. Amusingly, though sadly, it broke up over what he referred to as 'the cloths rota'. He explained, 'Just like her mother she was fastidious over housework to the point of having different coloured dishcloths for every different job – blue for the pans, white for the cutlery, pink for the plates, green for the table. No matter how much I tried I would always get it wrong and use the pink one for the pans, or the old green one for the windowsills when I should have been using it for the table. I

124

just couldn't stand it any more and couldn't see things getting any better, so I called it quits!'

Charlotte, a sophisticated, well-connected lady involved in the promotion of classical music was at a seventeenth century masked party in the French Consulate in Karachi, when a distinguished looking French diplomat caught her eye. Without delay she simply dropped the guy she had just been introduced to in mid-sentence, went up to the French man and said, 'Hullo, who are you? I'd like to meet you, you look interesting,' and later asked him to dance. She is a polite, self-effacing kind of woman so this behaviour was quite out of character. Perhaps the fact that she could hide behind the disguise gave her courage. The two of them hit it off immediately. At midnight they went for a romantic drive in the Sind desert, to the sound of Mozart concertos in stereo. For the first time in her life she had adventurously cut through all the slow, conventional rigmarole of placing herself strategically in order to be introduced. And it worked!

A fun evening was passed by all at the instigation of two decidedly liberated, and pretty, Sloany girls. An arty-looking Italian guy wearing a leather jacket, looking suitably dishevelled but 'cool', walked into a King's Road restaurant, briefly catching their eye. After giving him a few flirtatious glances they sent a message over, via the waiter: 'We would like to make your acquaintance.' Amused, he went over to ask them to join him and his friend at the table for a drink. This turned into a meal and later they all went on to a night club. At the end of the evening, the girls asked Mr Art-heart if he'd like to accompany them home to their Chelsea apartment. They didn't tell him what they had in store for him, which was a sex orgy involving all three of them. He had the time of his life. I am not advocating this type of behaviour but he was obviously interesting to them, and they made no fuss about getting what they wanted, all in the spirit of daredevil fun and amusement. I am sure it won't have done any of them any harm. NB I am assured that they were careful!

There is nothing wrong with making it perfectly clear that

you are open to meetings with new people. Everyone gets bored sometimes with their predictable social circle. You don't have to have anything more than a chat. You could even do this with a woman but between the sexes there is always that dash of excitement.

A scientific research assistant sent over a drink to an amiable looking chap in a wine bar who was dressed in a long bohemian style coat and a black hat. When he came over to thank her he said, 'What did I do to deserve this charming gesture?' She simply told him that she thought he looked interesting. Their friendship developed from there. By taking this bold step, which he found endearing, she ended up getting to know an illustrator who she would never have come across in her normal line of work or social life. Later that year she went on holiday with him to Istanbul.

Jessica, an aspiring film producer, met an editor through her work. She later called him up and invited him to a drinks party. When he asked which day she replied, 'Whichever day you like, Wednesday, Thursday, Friday . . . When are you free?' Evidently she hadn't arranged anything! They decided to make it the following Friday. Although he was only able to stay for twenty minutes on that particular evening she had given him enough encouragement to cause him to ask her out the following weekend. It was to make up for his short stay on the Friday, he said. A few months later they were engaged!

This is a perfect example of a successful, direct approach. Whilst in New York on business, James, a sprightly and confident barrister in his late twenties, went out to dinner on a blind date with Belle. The next day he received a fax from her, with a cartoon relating to a joke of the evening before but no message. He faxed an appropriate reply. Within minutes she called him to ask him out for a drink. They met at the top of the World Trade Centre building. Belle looked him straight in the face, 'There's no point in mucking around. I told my best friend that I've met the person I'd like to marry. Let's go out together for the next three months. Let's then be married and now let's kiss . . . I know that's not going to be a problem anyway.' Although he was keen on her already he was quite bowled over by her forthright approach. He said nothing. He was aware that she already had a boyfriend and so declined to pursue her passionate entreaty. In the back of the taxi he could resist her endearments no longer. They kissed, 'The most beautiful kiss ever, non-stop for twenty five minutes along Broadway.' As a lawyer he was particularly unaccustomed to losing control, so he still found her behaviour a cause for concern. As soon as he got back to London he called the person who originally put them in contact, to find out if Belle was normally as forthright as this to a man that she had only just met. He was assured that her pushy behaviour was totally out of character. In normal circumstances, being the perfect gentleman, he would have seen her every time he went to New York. For ages it would have remained merely a pussy footing flirtation caught between London, New York and her other boyfriend. As it was, Belle grabbed the bull by the horns and put herself point blank at his mercy or rather as he felt, the other way round! He wasn't strong enough to resist, nor did he really wish to resist the charm of such an earnest approach. This is his quote which has been seconded by a lot of men I have spoken to, 'It is undoubtedly a turn on for a man to be told he is liked and loved. He desperately needs reassurance of this. He adores the idea of being loved.' If you like him a lot don't hesitate to make your feelings known to him!

Destiny

I am talking about love at first sight. You can't search for this but you can create something out of such an auspicious meeting. Don't let opportunities slip you by, as so many people do.

There is always the possibility that the man your eyes are fixed upon may have been better left alone and remembered in the context of a beautiful moment. Often when you deign to speak to one another reality strikes and the magic evaporates. On the other hand when the attraction continues, that is always something worth satisfying your curiosity for!

Twenty-seven-year-old Edward gave up his job as a recording studio manager in order to join the Bhagwan cult in Amsterdam. On leaving a sports hall one afternoon after a game of squash, he vaguely recognised the young woman walking down the street towards him in connection with this same cult. It didn't really make any difference if he recognised her or not, because before he knew it he had stopped her to say, 'You are the most gorgeous person I've ever seen in my life.' Although she didn't recognise him she just flung her arms around him. They have lived together ever since, but have now moved to England, since he has returned to work in the music world.

A lithe male ballet dancer in his twenties walked out of the Urdang dance studios in London just as a thirty-year-old woman walked in. She was going to a jazz dance session. They simply looked at each other, never having set eyes on one another before, and fell in love. They spent the next two years together. It's not fair is it!

A single writer in her thirties was watching a band in a bar in Vancouver the evening before she returned to London. She described a kind of psychic experience: 'I felt somebody walking in behind me and I loved them. I knew where he was standing and I turned and saw this beautiful black man, radiant and appearing to me to have gold shining from his head.' They immediately started talking; he was a lawyer from Florida interested in giving his job up in order to concentrate on music. She went on, 'I have never before or after felt so relaxed with anyone. There was no sexual tension, we just got on so well. We spent the night together, but we both knew there was no future because we sensed that we knew everything about each other there was to know. It was almost as though we had met before.'

128

Opal, a twenty-six-year-old opera singer, was singing in the chorus of an Earl's Court production of *Carmen*. She was desperate to secure a more intimate meeting with Clive, a 'divine' young trendy author in the chorus, whom she had fallen madly in love with. Occasionally he gave her a lift to rehearsals but this wasn't the time to get to know him better. One day an opportunity afforded itself. As usual she was keeping him waiting because she was behind in getting ready. Out of the blue a football came smashing through her basement flat window. It had been thrown by some kids who promptly scarpered. Being a Sunday she couldn't get it mended and she was distressed at the thought of being left alone there. How was she, a poor, vulnerable little blonde girl, to last the night on her own, petrified of possible attackers? Not surprisingly, Clive seized the chance to offer his manly protection for the night. By the next morning it was perfectly clear to both of them that they were in love. After six months they are still inseparable.

Try running in Hyde Park. Crossing one another at the same spot, at the same time, for three consecutive days gave good reason for a couple of joggers to break for a chat. This is how Bonnie, who works for the Home Office, met and fell in love with an affluent American.

Love can strike at any age. The sweetest story I have heard concerns an embarrassed six-year-old girl who arrived for her first school term a few days later than everyone else. She was officially introduced to her class and captured the heart of a boy towards the back of the room. Luck was on his side as she was seated next to him. But how could he speak to her, he wondered? An idea came to light. Purposefully he dropped his pencil so it fell under her desk. He watched artfully. As she bent to pick it up he moved swiftly and simultaneously so their heads met. Then, once out of view of the teacher, he caused her to blush as he planted a rough kiss on her cheek. After marrying in their teens these two have remained together from that time to this, forty years later. She has

129

had plenty of work at home bringing up three kids but she earns a small independent income as a dressmaker. He became an RAF fighter pilot. But of course you can't ever contrive to find love at first sight, let alone at such a tender age!

SEVEN

The Professional Type: Mr Security

An Attractive Proposition

Mr Security is by definition an intelligent, respectable member of the community. He may be a doctor, lawyer, dentist, accountant, vet, architect or teacher. If you are contemplating him in the long term you can anticipate a quite high standard of living. He is often well rewarded indeed for his dedication and dependability. He is never likely to be out of work, which is a comforting thought. Most professions can be relocated easily as their services are in demand worldwide.

Essentially, Mr Security is paid to look after your best interests. I have been attracted to men who fall into this category because of their apparently caring and capable nature, as well as because they have helped me out of trouble at one time or another! At times you would think Mr Security is the only one who is concerned for you! You often find yourself in an intimate situation with Mr Security confiding your most personal physical, material or emotional problems. It is no wonder that a feeling of gratitude is common to many who successfully engage Mr Security's expertise. As a result he will have built up many friends and acquaintances from all walks of life, so there are endless opportunities for an interesting social life with him. He has position, status, and, as a conscientious professional, he should gather prestige and charisma with age, and that has to be a point worthy of consideration.

On the Negative Side

In the early years there is no steady cash flow. The qualifying period for most professions is anything between five and seven years, during which time Mr Security will almost inevitably be short of money, living on grants, and whatever money he can make in the holidays. He is also under the enormous pressure of exams. Bear in mind that there is a very high fall out rate, so don't count your chickens before they are hatched!

Mr Security's work carries a lot of responsibility. For doctors and vets this pressure is exacerbated by the fact that they are dealing with life and death situations and by their anti-social hours. Inevitably this can result in some of them becoming hardened and cynical. It can also result in alcohol abuse and ulcers.

As regards falling in love with a Mr Security who has helped you through a difficult time, you must always bear in mind that, in reality, your association of him with that bad period may dampen your enthusiasm in the future.

We tend to go to Mr Security in times of need, though whether we would if we were living with him is another matter. For example, many doctors are quite incapable of treating their own families. I knew of one doctor who was most reluctant to carry out his daughter's request and pierce her ears. He was so shaken after the event, one felt he deserved the St George's Cross! Neither should it be assumed that a talented chartered accountant will take care of the household accounts, nor that a solicitor will be any more rational than anyone else when someone accidentally smashes into his car. Many conscientious professionals confine their practice to within strict working hours, after which they feel free to drop their veneers and to be themselves!

You may find him a boring match. The nature of his responsible position means he is somewhat restricted by conventions which, if you become associated with him, you will have to respect too. For all that, Mr Security's good points undoubtedly outweigh the disadvantages of association with him – for most!

Meeting Mr Security on an Appointment

He may take your eye in a working situation, but, I stress, don't actually 'meet' him while he's in action, ie, in the surgery over the ingrowing toenails, or in the solicitor's office over a divorce suit. Flirtation distracts from the objective professional relationship, and from the quality of attention you can expect to receive. It is also clumsy and in poor taste though, God only knows, love knows no bounds! There are usually other people waiting, time is money and after all there is a job to do. Besides, putting on your knickers and socks and simultaneously chatting flirtatiously about the suntan that you picked up on your holiday in Turkey is incongruous, and not to be recommended.

Of course liaisons do sometimes start in these situations, such as in the case of a young hospital doctor I knew and a very attractive young woman patient. She literally collapsed at his feet in her nightie and he found her just too much to resist. Such liaisons are, however, strictly frowned upon by the professions and are restricted to total secrecy.

If you would like to get to know Mr Security better you must endeavour to do so in a different setting.

Is he Married?

First and foremost you should find out if your chosen Mr Security is married or not. One way of doing this is to call the centre of his operations under the guise of someone trying to get hold of his wife, her home address or her initial, in order, for instance, to send her some direct mail knitting pattern. Depending on the reply, ie, if you find out that he does in fact have a wife, well, you missed the boat, baby, and there is no need to proceed further!

All Clear

Supposing you should be so lucky as to find an unattached professional in the course of an appointment to whom you are attracted remember, by nature he is sociable and only too delighted to meet new people, but it won't be easy for him to ask you out in his professional capacity. He is strictly bound by a professional code of practice. Whether you reject him or not he risks being struck off, quite apart from losing you as a client, and laying himself open to damaging gossip. I mean, there is arguably something decidedly unsavoury about a lawyer who oversteps the mark by asking out the lady whose divorce he is trying to settle. On the whole, therefore, liaisons with professionals who you meet in a working situation can really only be initiated by you.

● Don't cringe in astonishment at this idea. You really don't have to be impertinent and pushy to do this. If he has been working on your behalf over a period of time, and you have developed some kind of rapport, why not ask him out for lunch to thank him for the good work he has done. See how this goes and take it from there. This is the first move, and even if you don't fall madly in love with him, you are at least in a position to get to know each other in a more natural situation. He is unlikely to refuse, for him it is public relations and public relations means business! I shall never understand why this isn't done more often. I am always eternally grateful for the help of these people.

● If he is local to you, or within easy access, ask him round for 'drinks'. This sounds quite unthreatening because it infers that there will be several people present. Added to which, it isn't so expensive! Perhaps you want to dispel the implication that you are 'after him', something a more intimate drink in the singular may quite accurately imply. If he can't make it you shouldn't feel slighted or embarrassed. Although you may feel disappointed, your ego shouldn't suffer!

● Buy an 'At Home' card from a stationers if you are too shy to ask Mr Security directly. Think up a pretext for a party – birthday celebration, Christmas, fun – and send him an invite on the card. This is an impersonal and acceptable means of invitation. If 'drinks' isn't your scene, though it can be made anyone's scene, really, then give a party. It may be a dinner party, which is always an attractive proposition or even a 'Bring a Bottle' party to which he could bring a friend. Perhaps the more casual the better, depending on his age. Obviously, if you are in, for instance, a delicate legal situation or recovering from an operation you are unlikely to be having parties but, where prudent, you shouldn't hesitate to ask him. Plausible reasons to give for inviting him are: to make up numbers; because you want to meet someone new; because you are having a big party and want as many people as you know to come to make it more interesting . . . and so forth.

The thing to do is grab the moment, even if you go to see a lawyer or an accountant just once. If you get on well tell him when you leave, 'I may be having a party, would you mind if I invited you?' Give one of the above reasons for inviting him – as you hardly know him – and then you don't risk too much by sending him an invitation. The worst that can happen is that he doesn't turn up, but the likelihood is that he will be flattered and will not hesitate to accept. He may well return the invitation at a later date.

Tips for Meeting Specific Professional Types

Architects

The **Architectural Association** in London is *the* venue for architects. Being one of the most prestigious centres for architects in the world, many trained architects frequent the building as well as students. The fees are very high so it attracts a wealthy, international range of students, about eighty per cent foreign and twenty per cent English. Enter the AA and ask for a list of the week's events. As a non-member of the AA you are welcome to attend most lectures and exhibitions. You can even attend some of the classes where work is being reviewed by peers and appraisals are being made. Following the classes the students usually trickle out to their hip and stylish bar for a drink, or for a bite to eat in the AA buffet. Why not join them? The stress is on style. Expensive, imaginative wardrobes abound.

Go to an exhibition of, for example, architectural drawings.

Ask the registrar to introduce you to the man responsible for an exhibit that you are interested in. The name of the architect is displayed beside the work – obviously look for a male name, if you can tell the difference with all those foreigners. Imply that you are writing an article or doing some research on the subject of the Spanish hinterland, or whatever area his work relates to. Architects do background work for all their projects, so conversation does not have to relate only to the technical side of the subject. You could pop in to do some work in the elegant and relaxed surroundings of the library. It doesn't take much to become familiar or to make friends: 'What stage of study are you at? Can I borrow a pen . . . ?'

The July carnival is the highlight of the year. This must be one of the most glamorous and trendy events of the summer in London. Just go along. You don't have to pay. It is open house. Strawberries and champagne are on tap. The place is full of the chic and glamorous and oozes with the trendiest of trendy artists, who all spill on to the square outside. Dishy, fledgling architects are never far from their work. Architectural drawings are nothing if not obscure to the untrained eye, so there is endless potential for conversation! For instance, ask him if he could begin to explain the particular drawing that you like the look of, but that you don't understand. His explanation may be incomprehensible, but it is a pleasure to listen to when swigged down flirtatiously with champagne!

Barristers and Solicitors

Popular Haunts in London

Lawyers, like many other men in the city, work so hard that they simply don't have the time to give to a social life – which doesn't mean that they aren't interested in women! Every male lawyer I have spoken to has expressed great enthusiasm for the idea of a woman making herself known to him. He simply doesn't come across them enough during his working day, and in the evening he is too flaked to involve himself in enterprising social activities.

138

The many bars and pubs around Chancery Lane such as the Duke of York pub, The Cock Tavern on Fleet Street, the Devereux Pub on Devereux Street or the Roundhouse pub on Garrick Street are a haven for solicitors, barristers, and for graduates at the Council of Legal Education who are doing their one year Bar finals. It is not unknown, nor a problem, for a couple of girls to find their way into the bars which belong to the respective Inns of Court. These are essentially non-academic colleges for barristers with a dining hall, library and common rooms. You may be able to find your way into the common rooms, although theoretically you should go in as a friend or guest of one of the barristers. Debates and all manner of social and academic activities are organised here.

The Stage
Barristers cut dashing figures, working as articulate, eloquent, and flamboyant mouthpieces on the stage of justice. Fond of their own voices, they have a predilection for acting and singing. This is catered for in the singing and acting groups run by the Inns of Court. They are frequently looking for outsiders to make up numbers. Information about these groups can be found on the various notice boards about the place.

Chapel Concerts
Alternatively you can listen to, or participate in, any of the concerts in the chapel in the Inner Temple. Once you have befriended someone here, the interest you've shown in the people and the activities on campus should lead to invitations to the annual inns of court balls such as the Inner Temple Autumn ball and other social events. You are also likely to receive an invitation to lunch in one of the magnificent oak-panelled dining rooms – an experience in itself.

Dinner Parties
Dinner parties are number one meeting grounds for lawyers. Being on the whole articulate, barristers and solicitors are at ease to chatter, their favourite pastime, and charm with

139

their gift of the gab. If you are ever short of conversation ask him about the most interesting case he has dealt with, or is dealing with. The role of raconteur is his forte!

Balls
For lawyers' charity balls you will need a contact in order to secure an invitation. For the Inns' balls you don't need to know anyone if you are prepared to invest in the ticket. Tickets are available from the respective Inns and cost in the region of £75 per head. To get the most out of the occasion it is best to go with a few people.

Social Issues
Fresh, conscientious lawyers who are actively engaged in pressing social issues are interesting. They may for instance be involved in the creation and development of environmental law or the law of human rights, or in the revision of the present cumbersome tangle of law. The best way of meeting any of these men is to become actively involved through voluntary work in, for example:

    a The local Conservation Association.
    b The **National Council of Civil Liberties**
    c The **Haldane Society of Socialist Lawyers**
    d Your neighbourhood Law Centre.
    e **Amnesty International**

The Citizens' Advice Bureau will be able to help with some address information.

The Medics

Doctors tend to be available either when they are very young at college or when they are learning the ropes in hospitals. In some cases they re-emerge divorced when they are older, the wife having tired of their often unreasonable working hours. Needless to say, many doctors marry other doctors or nurses. There are obvious practical advantages in their similar routines. There is always someone with medical knowledge available to answer the phone, particularly useful with a GP, and they share mutual interests. Even so, there are opportunities for those without a medical background – you can always catch up on that later!

- Medical colleges are frequently isolated from other disciplines, so seek them out. Find out the local haunts of the young medics, ie, the local pubs, and meet them here or involve yourself in their college activities. Look on their noticeboards. Young doctors, dentists, and vets frequently have a ribald sense of humour. Join their university rags and fancy-dress parties, though bear in mind that they are not for the faint-hearted. Some of their humour is explicit, to say the least! Forget the bedside manner, that comes later – one way or another!

- While visiting a patient in hospital or on the pretext perhaps of perusing the hospital noticeboard for ways to contribute to patients' welfare, you may choose to get lost in one of the corridors until you come across a dishy enough medic to point you in the right direction. Alternatively ask for the doctors' quarters, a sort of common room rest area with canteen. If anyone asks you any questions tell him/her that you are looking up someone who you used to go to school with. Doctors will be only too happy to meet a healthy woman with fresh conversation to tide them over the break. Public hospital canteens are another stopping off point for him, probably to have a change of company from all those in the doctors' quarters!

- Divorced doctors frequently need help coping with children. A good way to meet them is to offer your services as a temporary, or permanent, housekeeper, via an advertisement in a magazine or newspaper such as the *Lady*, *The Times* or the *Telegraph*: or even in a doctor's journal such as the *Lancet* or the *British Medical Journal*. Doctors, as with most professional men, need to keep up a calm, well ordered front, even though all hell may be let loose behind the scenes! Once living under the same roof, even if you and he don't hit it off, there will be a constant influx of medical friends and associates visiting. The disadvantage of this situation is that he may become jealous if he fancies you, and you don't want involvement. In frustration he may adopt a dog in the manger attitude to anyone else who has a liking for you.

Vets

Vets encourage any interest and enthusiasm shown towards animals. At your local practice ask if you can accompany one of the vets on his rounds for a few weeks or days, or even over a few weekends if you work during the week. Such a possibility is not only restricted to veterinary students. You could always use the experience with a view to future work in the practice. A particularly interesting round to make would be with those vets who deal with zoo animals or, if you are interested in horses, those well paid vets who specialise in the treatment of race horses! Vets are often isolated in their work and so are likely to be appreciative of company. In time you would become familiar with the rest of the vets in the practice.

Clergymen

If the caring and committed hands of a clergyman interests you the best place to find him is of course in church, away from the rush and hurly burly of everyday life. Remember, he always shakes your hand as you leave! By visiting churches, chapels and other denominations, you will have the opportunity to meet clergymen as well as to make many friends along the way! Coffee mornings are an ideal meeting place and what about sporting your new hat at his annual garden party! Talks and lectures may prove fortuitious occasions. There is plenty of room for theological debate in which you can participate, or if you find that idea intimidating, then ask him questions at the end, alone, over a cup of coffee.

Become a Sunday school teacher, offer to help with the church flowers, join the committee that raises money for church funds. Brass rubbing is a worthwhile interest to take up. The materials are inexpensive and the technique is simple. Ask permission from your local clergyman and get him interested in it!

Church choirs are ideal for meeting clergymen. Pippa, a shy school teacher with a pleasant voice, joined a choir and she was lucky enough to fall in love with a lay preacher there. Many years later they are still very happily married.

Teachers

The guiding role of a school master, who is responsible for the education and discipline of children, is not to be sneezed at. One of the greatest attractions, although he will dispute this point, are his long holidays, especially if you would like to go on adventurous trips abroad. Other professions rarely afford such freedom.

• Meet him at school. Staff rooms are a hub of social activity, together with the local pubs of course. Temporary jobs are comparatively simple for anyone to find in a boarding or prep school. Teachers are absent sometimes, as in other professions, because of pregnancy or illness. Someone is then needed to fill in during the interim period. An aptitude for a subject such as art, French or sports may well be all that you need in order to offer your services. Look in the *Times Educational Supplement* and local papers. Telephone the schools and offer your services.

Twenty-six-year-old Jemma filled in an emergency vacancy for a maths teacher in a boys' prep school. Her novel teaching experience led to a delightful romance with Jeremy, another temporary teacher. Together with other members of staff, she was amused by the low IQ of the school dog, a fat Spaniel called Salty. Jeremy was about to become a clergyman and Jemma learned that he had purchased a hearse, but that he had nowhere to park it. His parents wouldn't allow it in sight of their house and the neighbours were similarly outraged when he moved it to outside their house. Jemma was entertained by this problem and couldn't resist doodling

143

a cartoon of Salty peeing up the wheel of the hearse. She left it, unsigned, on his desk. Jeremy, guessing the identity of the artist, retaliated with a drawing of her pushing her own ancient vehicle with Salty watching! And so began their affair!

● Apart from teaching there are many other ways of getting into a school. Perhaps you can cook, or type, or help with domestic tasks. Matrons and assistants are often needed. Maybe you are a good driver and can offer your services on an occasional basis. A young woman called Anne became a nanny to the headmaster's children, and left on the arm of the music teacher. Once ensconced in the daily running of a school the opportunities are endless.

● Why not go to the school directly and ask around for private lessons in something such as history, mathematics, or whatever subject you would like to brush up on — human biology perhaps! Alternatively, ask him whether he could advise you on where to find information on a particular project you have undertaken. There are plenty of pretexts for returning for some more help or advice. School secretaries will inform you about who teaches what, and if you probe a little deeper they are sure to give a brief description of the staff.

● Infant school teachers are glad of craft materials, as are art departments. If you have hundreds of yoghurt pots, cardboard rolls or similar, take them along as an excuse to introduce yourself. Sort out something interesting from your attic, the skeleton of a beaver for the biology department, or dressing up clothes for the teacher who looks after the wardrobe for the drama group. Involvement in schools is encouraged, so it won't be awkward becoming familiar with the staff room.

● As with most people, male teachers are flattered at being asked to divulge their knowledge on a particular subject, so go to the school on the pretext of picking his brains. Then take him a small gift in thanks, or invite him for a drink or coffee. As teachers finish work earlier than most —

between three and four-thirty pm – catch him just before he leaves.

General Haunts

Sports Clubs

You will find professional men engaged in sociable sports such as golf, tennis, squash – and drinking! Obviously it is a great benefit to be of a sporty disposition. There is nothing like a few rounds of golf or a hard game of tennis for getting to know people.

Become a member of a local sports club or, if you want to be sure of bumping into your own Mr Security, ask his advice on any sports clubs in the area that he would recommend. Knowing that professionals are quite informative on this subject you thought it worthwhile asking him! He is likely to have some ideas and may well suggest his own club, particularly if you are of similar ages, and Bob's your uncle! Alternatively, call all the clubs in the area and ask if he is one of their members. Clubs will, and do, admit this much about their membership.

If you think this amount of research is going overboard take a tip on perseverance from Yvette, a twenty-four-year-old American. On arriving at a popular disco in New York with her boyfriend she proceeded to fall out with him. As a consequence of their dispute she got drunk, whereupon her boyfriend left her for the night. In spite of the unpleasant start to the evening she was nonetheless determined to enjoy herself and so she started dancing with another man who had taken her eye. Soon, however, the drink got the better of her and she made a bolt for the ladies. Unfortunately for the man she didn't make it and threw up all over him instead! It wasn't until the next day when she woke up, and the events of the night before started coming back to her, that she realised she was indebted to this man for having taken care of her and for having made sure that she got home safely. Despite the fact that she didn't have his telephone number, nor did she know what area of town he came from, she made

145

up her mind to contact him in order to apologise and to thank him for helping her. She only remembered his name – Justin Stern – although she wasn't even sure of that. Thus she had to call every person in New York with a similar name until she found him, giving his description in the hope he was someone's son or nephew. After two days on the phone she tracked him down, to some effect as the couple have now been married to each other for five merry years!

Conversation about sport is a good way to break the ice. If he is a golfing enthusiast for instance, and you don't play, explain that you would like to learn. Maybe he will offer to give you some lessons in his own plush club. Ask if he would like to go to a golfing tournament. Your excuse is that you have a spare ticket, someone let you down and you don't know anyone else interested in golf – ho ho!

General Pastimes

Popular pastimes for Mr Security are bridge, chess and dramatic clubs. They are an ideal form of escapism and are favourable for meetings on a regular basis. You can find out about these either on your local library noticeboard or in your local newspaper or through the **English Bridge Union** or **British Chess Federation**.

University Faculties and Professional Colleges

Go to university/college canteens or bars, or to pubs in the vicinity. Look on the noticeboards about the place for activities which you can join in such as sports, dances and open lectures. Judy and Sarah, two young Surrey prep school teachers, used to find out when a university party was on in London and go together. Both of them met their husbands this way – a law and an economics undergraduate respectively. University as opposed to private parties are usually advertised on noticeboards and in the college rag magazine.

Advertise your typing or word processing services privately, in a student newspaper or on a college noticeboard. Wait until you meet him before quoting rates – if he's your sort of guy keep them low, if he's not, well, that's up to you!

Professional Bookshops

Go into specialist bookshops, or at least the departments of large bookshops that specialise in a profession that you are interested in. Ask whoever is browsing there and takes your eye something like this:

● Law – I'm looking for a specialist in the law of professional negligence, or another arresting topic. Then you can explain why.

● Veterinary – I wonder if you could point me in the right direction for a book on illnesses relating to donkeys/tortoises/cats ... or whatever animal takes your fancy! Do you know of a vet who deals with reptiles? I'm thinking of buying a python and I'm not sure if it is a good idea ... That should set you off on a conversation!

● 'Architect – Are you in the architecture and design world?' Assuming he says yes, go on; 'I need some help on how to design a studio for my house. I wonder if you could point me in the right direction ... ?'

● Chartered Accountant. 'Do you have the time?'

● Doctors – 'I'm trying to find out doctors' opinions on homeopathic medicine, perhaps you could help me ... ?'

● Dentists – While he's musing over the intracacies of modern dentistry introduce yourself with, 'I've always been fascinated to know if dentists ever get bored with dentistry,' and smile!

● Teachers – They are not so easy to identify but you may find them musing over school textbooks. Ask him something like, 'What would be the best way to get lessons organised for myself in remedial maths?'!

Libraries

Get to know your library. Libraries are great hunting grounds for professionals, who frequent them both for work and for pleasure. Do as Patricia, a fun and intelligent thirty-year-old did. First locate your book in a lonely corner on a rather

147

obscure subject, and then sidle up to an intelligent looking man. Her chosen man was John, an affluent-looking, if portly, chartered accountant. She asked if he could possibly help her to find a particular book, ie, the one she had seen earlier. John, a man of the world, needed no second bidding. He found the book, they chatted and their affair began. Librarians shouldn't have much problem making conversation with lone Securities who take their eye while perusing the bookshelves. Note that doctors and clergymen frequently like whodunnits and murder mysteries, presumably as a form of escapism! You only have to comment on the book or books he has chosen to provoke conversation, and there is the chance to see him again when he returns them!

Reading rooms in libraries, though usually quiet, give the opportunity for conversations to take place. Comment on a topical subject that you have just read about. Ask the time. Ask to borrow a pen/paper. Show interest in the book he is reading or has got next to him. Ask whether he knows where a certain magazine is, drop a file of papers. Get yourself noticed!

Charity Balls

These kind of social do's attract many professionals. Save up for a ticket. They are also usually advertised in society magazines like *Tatler* and *Harpers & Queen*. Alternatively send off to a **charity organisation** for a ticket. It will normally be followed by a host of invitations to other charity balls. Remember that lots of people go with partners purely because it is obligatory to balance numbers. Don't be put off by that. It doesn't stop you from mixing when you are there. Folks are often just dying for an opportunity to ditch their partner!

When you meet the intriguing Mr Security here, be careful what you talk about. Remember to separate his profession from his personality. Don't keep nervously talking about how interesting his profession must be. Keep off the subject of how much a five digit gold bridge costs in London compared with Birmingham, or how long the waiting list was for your cat's hysterectomy operation. Don't be tempted to ask questions that you would normally be paying a fee for either. He needs to be able to break away from the office, to spend his well earned money! So although a healthy and respectful interest is appreciated, no professional will be inspired by talking for very long about his work. He is one of the unusual characters in this book who would probably be just as interested in pure flirtation, in hearing about you, and about what you are doing, as opposed to talking about himself.

EIGHT

Travelling Tips:
Mr Traveltrip

What better way to meet an interesting man than by travelling? There are a few points to consider. First, in the process of brightening up your life, you will make yourself a more interesting and attractive proposition for a man. Staying put may well have couched you in parochial English attitudes and complacency. Put yourself in gear before it is too late! Second, Mr Traveltrip comes from another world to you and thus, by definition, he is interesting. He is on the move and although in the short term he won't be around for long, for some reason meetings that take place while travelling are often memorable occasions, and of enough significance to lead to romances and long-lasting friendships. Sometimes there is nothing to stop you from joining him on your travels. Thirdly, travelling is a great equaliser. It overcomes differences that might otherwise have come between you if you had been on home territory. Here are some tips and lines of encouragement to set you on your way.

Cheap hotels and Youth Hostels

These are ideal, neutral venues for meeting travellers of all ages – incidentally they are not all hitchhikers. It's not luxury accommodation but it is clean. In youth hostels you are protected by the segregated sleeping arrangements, so you can yack to Mr Traveltrip in the common room until all hours, without feeling under pressure. However, if you meet English men this way, try to steer the conversation away from the dismal dialogue of how much your ticket cost and from which bucket shop you bought it. It has got to be the biggest turn-off. England looms too close for comfort!

This is an example of the effortless sort of meeting I am talking about. Mary and Teresa, two carefree girls on holiday from a catering firm based in Sussex, went down to breakfast one morning in a youth hostel in San Diego. They smiled at a kindly looking chap sipping coffee, who wished them good morning. On hearing his English accent they started chatting to him. He was a law lecturer from London who had taken a six-month break to see America and boost his flagging morale. Although he was heading in the direction of the Grand Canyon that day he postponed his trip in order to give them a lift to see whales in the Pacific. They subsequently became close friends during the trip. On his return to England he contacted Mary in particular, and spent a good deal more time with her. She had, after all, used his practised powers of articulation to draft a goodbye letter to her ex-boyfriend to explain that it was all over between them.

If you travel alone for any length of time you tend to get sick of your own company. The idea of getting a friendly knock on your hotel door to ask if you'd like to go out for a drink may not appeal to you now, but the chances are that were you in that situation you'd jump at the opportunity. Indeed, there is nothing to stop you doing the knocking. Pauline, a twenty-six-year-old quality control supervisor from Leicester, was travelling in Burma. After travelling for three months around China she wasn't going to blush at the thought of introducing herself to anyone. She knocked at the door of a tall, fresh-faced Englishman with attractively tousled, wavy hair, who she had seen enter the hotel earlier in the afternoon with a few maps and a book under his arm. Over a couple of glasses of the local brew at a nearby tavern they decided to join forces and explore the area. Subsequently they went on to spend several weeks in Kashmir together.

You could put an advertisement in a *Youth Hostel* magazine (or contact the **British Youth Hostel Association**) for someone to accompany you on a particular expedition. You never know, something may turn up in the *Castaway* vein – though I am not advising marriage for the sake of adventure!

By Air

Once you have decided that you are going to travel, it is worth investigating the relative costs of transport to more exotic destinations than you had perhaps contemplated at first. For instance, a couple of weeks of trekking around Nepal is likely to cost less than a month in Sweden, including the air fare. *The Round The World Air Guide* by Katie Wood is a useful book to start with. Here are some worthwhile tips along your route by plane.

● When you check in ask if it is possible to be put next to a dishy bloke on his own! I have known men who regularly request a seat next to a good-looking woman when they travel Club Class.

● Board the plane after everyone else. If it is not too crowded and you have the nerve, ask a man who takes your eye if the seat next to him is taken. If it is not, sit down next to him. Margaret, a bubbly American advertising executive, approached a handsome young man in this way. He was a male model flying from Paris to New York. By coincidence it turned out that he lived on the same street as her in New York. By the time they arrived they had made a date and they continued dating for a good many months afterwards.

● Always put yourself down for an aisle seat rather than the more popular window seat. It gives you a choice of people to talk to – two on your left and one on your right. If one of your neighbours is boring, you may have better luck over the way. You can always lean over to have a look at the view!

It doesn't take much to start a conversation, perhaps only a smile. In the case of Holly, a vital and imaginatively dressed teacher returning from a visit to her brother in Spain, she used her sense of humour to turn an embarrassing situation in her favour. The man next to her, a graphic designer, was struck with a bout of uncontrollable sneezing which made her giggle. After plying him with tissues their conversation led him to invite her to an exhibition he was organising. The subsequent meeting blossomed into an affair lasting a good few years.

Louise, a refined English nanny, was flying out to her job in Hong Kong. Exhausted, she fell asleep on the shoulder of the dishy man to her left — no doubt accidentally on purpose! The lucky guy was a racing driver on his way to Australia via Singapore. After several meetings with him in Singapore, she made her own independent trip to India and the Himalayas before returning to settle with him in Australia. Maybe you could contrive to do the same. You could even take a sedative to knock you out and create a genuine impression of sleep! After making a mental note of whose shoulder you would like to fall on just let yourself drift off!

There is something to be learned from this story. Nadia, an elegant French girl, was travelling back from Strasbourg with her pompous English lover, whose nose was boringly immersed in the *Financial Times*. She smiled shyly in resignation, and chatted to the handsome Traveltripper next to her — a little footsie footsie was thrown in to make the journey entirely bearable! On landing at Heathrow, to the English man's horror, he recognised through the plane's porthole his wife and mother-in-law waiting smugly on the spectators' balcony to catch him out. They had obviously found out about his French mistress, formerly the family au pair! While he panicked, Nadia took charge of the situation and, with French adroitness, took the arm of the handsome young man who she had been flirting with and asked him if he would mind if she left the plane with him. Like that it looked as if it was purely coincidental that they happened to be on the same plane together! Weeks later, when her official lover called unexpectedly at her apartment, he noticed a vaguely familiar face on a photograph next to her bed! Quick thinking eh!

Take addresses as a matter of course, like Americans do

154

at parties, and follow them up, no matter how much later. It is a great way to broaden your social and amorous horizons!

On her departure from Montreal to London, Diana, a shapely twenty-two-year-old Canadian marketing consultant, was heartbroken. She wasn't going to see her boyfriend for at least six months while she was away travelling in Europe. Lo and behold, she was distracted an hour into the flight by someone she described as, 'A divine young man with heavenly eyes.' He caught her attention as he got up to go to the loo. Without hesitation she went up to the man sitting next to him and asked very nicely if he would mind swopping seats with her. He kindly obliged, so that when the man she fancied returned, he found Diana sitting next to him. She introduced herself with, 'You look like Bruce Springsteen, would you mind talking to me . . . ?' He didn't turn out to be as exciting as Bruce Springsteen but this spontaneous move satisfied her curiosity and earned her a useful contact in England. Besides, it distracted her from pining for her boyfriend in Canada!

James, a successful property developer in his late twenties, was returning home from the States. Despite his spruce appearance he was feeling utterly dejected, having just broken off with the love of his life. When the cheery chap sitting next to him nudged him and exclaimed, 'Wow, just take a look at her', his eyes following a trim, young stewardess with long, strawberry-blonde hair and swinging hips, James hadn't much choice but to throw her a cursory glance, although he was far from in the mood to be eyeing up women. A little later another hostess, who was clearing away James' lunch plate, mischievously enquired whether he had found something on his tray. Surprised, he looked again and found a note which had obviously been carefully placed there earlier. It read, 'I think you are one of the best things that's walked onto the plane.' He smiled and promptly replied by note, via the hostess, 'Thanks very much for the compliment but I've never been called a thing before.' He was surprised, though impressed, by such a novel approach,

155

and smiling to himself he thought, good luck to her. Half an hour later and somewhat bored with the in-flight film, he took the opportunity to seek out his mystery admirer! She turned out to be the pretty strawberry-blonde hostess who had been pointed out to him by his neighbour earlier on. Depressed as he was, and with nothing to lose now that he had split up with his girlfriend, he arranged to see her during the week. Despite what you may think, far from being a brazen man-eater she is in fact quite a shy woman by nature. She placed the note there more as a dare than anything else. Her success was celebrated at their expense when the captain, having heard of the ruse, announced over the loudspeaker, 'All the crew would just like to congratulate Penny on the announcement of her engagement this morning!' Her playful initiative caught Mr Traveltrip quite unawares and has led to their recent, genuine engagement.

Trains

● Train rides provide an excellent opportunity for meetings. Sitting next to, or opposite, a stranger for a few hours often leads to some sort of verbal exchange. The beauty of trains is that unless you have reserved a seat you can choose who to sit next to.

Lorna, a bright red-headed student, started talking to the dishy man opposite her on the long train journey down from Edinburgh to London. He opened their conversation by asking her where she was studying. He turned out to lead an interesting life as a North-Sea diver. After a couple of hours they stopped talking, at which point she asked if she could borrow a pen. She began to jot ideas down on paper and then fell asleep, pen in hand. The man had gone when she woke up, but later that week she was surprised to see a note on her college notice board which read, 'Would red-headed girl on the train down from Edinburgh to London like to return biro? If so please call this number.' She did call him and they met once again. She continues to see him from time to time when he is down in London.

Jane, a bubbly twenty-five-year-old Welsh girl who had given up her secure administrative job in order to lend her life some excitement, was travelling to Rome by train. She was joined in the sleeper train in Paris by a charming Anglo-Italian guitarist who she described as, 'The epitome of the dashing artist'. They made friends quickly and after a while she opened a little flask of whisky. She invited him to toast her new found freedom — at least that was her story! By the time they reached Lyon a romantic adventure was well under way. It made no odds to them that they were joined here by four Americans. I am sure that this is not the first time that love and desire have alighted on the sleeper speeding through the night across France, Switzerland and northern Italy! So a piece of advice which may serve you well is to remember to carry a dram of something warming to bring out at an opportune moment!

● Try commenting on the headlines of the newspaper that Mr Traveltrip is reading and get into a political debate, as did a divorced lady in her thirties on a Surrey train. The discussion became so heated that it had to be continued when they reached their destination. And so she made friends with a highly interesting man who, apart from anything else, had been a news reporter in Vietnam and was a successful science-fiction writer. Interesting was not the word!

● Appear lost and frail and ask for directions or where you can leave your baggage, or best of all where to get a coffee. Then Mr Traveltrip might join you!

This story has a twist, but the principle of how I met and became friends with my Mr Traveltrip is the same. I was returning from a few days in Chantilly by hovercraft. Bad weather had delayed the journey so I took a coffee up against the bar next to a stylish young man who turned to me and asked the time in French. Detecting an accent, I asked him if he was English, which he was, of course, and we then conversed non-stop to Dover. It transpired that he was returning from his sculpture exhibition in Paris to resume studies at Cambridge University. After boarding the London-bound train, it seemed that there was still time for him to nip off and buy us some coffee before the train left. Unfortunately, this wasn't so. I was soon heading towards London without him but accompanied by all his luggage. We had been talking so much that we hadn't exchanged names so I looked in his jacket pocket for identification. To my astonishment I discovered he was a boy who had been at school with me and from whom I had once received a fine, hand-made Valentine card. The young fifteen-year-old that I remembered had matured beyond recognition into a charming and desirable young man. On meeting him at the lost property office later I asked him if he knew who I was. He had indeed known within a couple of minutes of first speaking to me, but hadn't let on for his amusement!

Backpacking

Marilyn, a vivacious and pleasant looking twenty-eight-year-old from California, was backpacking through Europe and had made England her first port of call. She was sitting in a Wimpy Bar at Kings Cross station eating breakfast when her eyes alighted on a smartly dressed young man. He saw that he had aroused her interest and encouraged her with typical English coldness – a stony glance quickly diverted towards an even more avid reading of the paper as he turned the page. Well, she was quite amused by this display of the native reserve that English men are so renowned for, and she drew a little closer towards him saying, 'What is in the news today?' She read out the headlines, 'Deerby day?', the pronunciation of which he corrected. Encouraged by his bluntness, she went on to lie through her teeth in the hope that he would return to the Wimpy if he was interested in her. She said that she went there every day for breakfast. Sure enough, the next day, though a little later than expected, they met again and made a date. She continued on her travels up to Scotland and he later joined her in Greece. They are now married and live in England: she is an account executive for a packing company and he works for a manufacturing firm.

Here is yet another example of an interesting meeting which happened while travelling. Shared humour acts as a natural bond: Hilary, a scruffily dressed Australian freelance journalist, was returning to Australia from her backpacking travels in Europe via Cairo and the Far East. While in Cairo she went to a *Son et lumière* show, at a venue overlooking the Pyramids. She sat down next to a friendly, bright-eyed, bearded chap, who was ordering a gin and tonic for himself. Within minutes the two of them were reeling in fits of laughter over the crass commentary which was coming over the loudspeaker. He was a twenty-seven-year-old export-import specialist. Luckily for her, he also had a chauffeur waiting downstairs who was able to take them both for a romantic dinner in town.

Shelley, an Irish girl with long, dark plaits and fair skin, was travelling on a tram in Amsterdam. She sat down next to a young man with a backpack and said, 'I thought you looked interesting.'

He replied, 'I'm really glad that you came down to sit next to me . . .' It was only a ten minute ride before she had to get off, but time enough for them to exchange numbers. After two years of wandering the continent as a writer the man was on his last couple of weeks of freedom before returning to America. The result of this brief meeting was that they maintained regular correspondence over the next couple of months, culminating in a trip together to Las Vegas and a driving holiday through the Utah desert.

Travelling, even if it's only for a week, is stimulating and boosts enthusiasm for life. It takes you out of your world and puts your everyday worries into perspective. Perhaps most uplifting of all is that the people you meet when you are travelling communicate with you at face value about the adventure in hand rather than pigeon-holing you according to your situation at home. Travelling presents a great opportunity to practise taking the initiative, because if ever you fail, the chances are that you will never see the man in question again!

NINE

Gold Diggers Anonymous: Mr Moneybags

Money affords the means to live a charmed and interesting life. It is power, and power is a turn-on. Like a hallucinogenic drug that can turn an ant into a giant, the possession of a lot of money creates the illusion in the minds of many that the man who has it is of more significance than the man who does not. Mr Moneybags' girlfriend or wife is seen by many to uphold the illusion!

Forewarned is forearmed. I have spent a lot of time on the case for and against wanting to meet a rich man, and on his ideal woman. Mr Moneybags is highly sought after, thus some understanding of him and of what he has to offer is essential to put you ahead of other female contenders for his attention. Once you know who you are up against and your mind is made up that Mr Moneybags is the man for you, or at least the kind of man that you want to meet, then there should be little problem in successfully making a go of it. Perhaps one day, in the not too distant future, you will be able to do the same as the girl in *Gentlemen Prefer Blondes*: play your line and tease him to spend his money on the greatest investment of all, yourself. He will be forever grateful for the meaning you have given to his life!

I have played devil's advocate throughout this chapter. I must underline the fact that the conclusions I have given on how to meet him are a result of research and my own observations, but I don't necessarily approve of all of them!

The Entrepreneur

I advise you to look out for the entrepreneur. The criterion for meeting Mr Moneybags is his money, but you may as well angle for the most interesting sort of Moneybags within this category. I would say that the entrepreneur is one of the most exciting, intriguing, and therefore intrinsically interesting characters as a whole. He is a self-starter who turns his own original ideas into commercially viable propositions. He is impassioned with the desire to make a lot of money and, to this end, he singlemindedly uses his imagination, his wits and his intuition. He is prepared to take high risks in order to pursue any particular project, but this optimistic, energetic man has usually calculated the risks very carefully. The rewards he stands to gain if everything goes well are too high to brush aside. Mr Moneybags, the entrepreneur, is above all a survivor. He is not afraid of failure. He believes only in himself. A fast and powerful motor car commonly seems to be the hallmark of his achievements.

An Attractive Proposition

There is the buzz of conquest. If you have the sexual power to hold the attention of a man of wealth and kudos, you are likely to feel a certain pride. To be on the arm of a very important man must make you feel desirable, valuable and, most of all, enviable. You are almost bound to feel important, albeit that it is an essentially false sense of your own importance.

If you fall in love with a rich man, or more to the point if he falls in love with you, his wealth will be at times an exhilarating potion which will bring you spontaneity, travel, interesting company and luxury. No longer will you be left to hover just out of reach of all these material goodies wishing 'if only'. There will be the thrill of St Moritz in the winter, Marrakesh in the summer; his investment in bigger and bigger diamonds every year, probably in order to assuage his two-timing conscience! Most husbands can't promise this type of consolation. In effect, you will have reached the pot of gold at the end of the rainbow.

With the assistance of Mr Moneybags you may choose to live as a lady of leisure in society. In other words, his wealth with scarcely any housekeeping for bringing up their three children.

For Mr Moneybags, getting something for nothing, including you, is probably one of his greatest turn-ons in life — if not the greatest turn on! But for you this distasteful, penny-pinching meanness may turn out to be the biggest turn-*off*. If you think you can pick up on the challenge of trying to change him, you are on a million to one loser. Who knows, his meanness may be an indication of his passion in the bedroom too!

'Are you ever bothered by the fact that women might be more attracted to your money, than to you as a person?' I asked a glamorous young advertising art director.

He paused for thought, shrugged his shoulders and smiled; 'Not really.' And he wasn't the only one. I admired his honesty but he makes the point that, like many a beautiful woman, he is aware of the power of his attraction and is prepared to use it to get what he wants. So, if you find yourself taking your clothes off in his Ferrari one evening, don't begin to confuse him in your mind with a knight in shining armour; the chances are, he is not. The probability is that you are using this fantasy to veil the fact that you are being seduced by whatever you think he has to offer, which may be no more or no less than a good time in a great car!

Mr Moneybags is frequently a workaholic, and workaholics are more of a menace than another woman! Time means money but time also means a relationship with both of you and any children. Beware of slipping into the passive role of Mr Moneybags' girlfriend, or wife! The dregs of his time may only afford you a thin wash of mawkish affection now and then, to keep you quiet. It is not enough. As a father his contribution to the children's development may only be about two hours a week on the odd Sunday. He will no doubt have their photo on his desk, but he will leave the house in the morning before they are up and return after they are in bed.

In a competitive world the following situation may be

understandable but it is nonetheless unforgiveable. A young woman I spoke to, who worked in a London office, met a film producer who was just starting his own business. It was one of the few occasions that he had found time to go to a party. It was love at first sight. They walked towards each other and were locked together in conversation for the rest of the evening. Unfortunately, it was a love affair nipped in the bud by the demands he allowed his work to make upon him. The final score was that they went out together only six times in eight months. If rich and busy Mr Moneybags does not spend enough time with you, then it is no wonder that you might start looking elsewhere for attention!

Several guys in this category have told me that they would not marry a beautiful woman because they could not stand the fact that everywhere she went, 'Men would want to screw her'. I have similar thoughts about a rich man being a target for all women. So concentrate on the job or you may get very hurt. Remember why you are after this guy. It is for a comfortable, indulgent lifestyle and not necessarily a meaningful relationship.

It is likely to be Mr Moneybags' show, not a shared one. They say that behind every great man there is an even greater woman. However, you have to ask yourself whether you could put up with the nonsense of him taking all the credit for your ideas, in order to keep his ego buoyant. For example, you suggest, 'It'd be a good idea to invest in a cottage in Tuscany, darling Dickie.' The next day at a dinner party you hear him saying, 'I've been thinking of investing in a house in Tuscany for the family,' as though you hadn't even heard about it, let alone suggested it!

If Mr Moneybags is generous, you are open to attack; 'The stupid bitch is only with him for his money.' And if he is stingy, and you are not demanding enough, you are likely to be looked upon as *just* his girlfriend or his wife or even a colourless alcoholic appendage if you are not careful!

Mr Moneybags likes glitter in the form of fast cars, investments and women – probably in that order. Who wants to because I had my hair up/down/it's been cut . . .' One of the girls looks down at her glass which is purposefully running on empty and is offered a drink by one of the guys. Thus they are all set for the evening. This method is a little dangerous, especially if you are usually honest, but remember the most honest people make the best liars. The point is that you have managed to break the ice and even if there is no pretext to talk again with them that evening, there may well be a pretext in the future – without deceit!

• Stay sober but encourage Mr Moneybags to drink. The intention is to break down his inhibitions and get him to confide in you – a classic hostess trick but good value!

Wealthy Haunts

As life tends to deal the wealthy out in one hand, that is to say the rich are naturally socially lumbered with one another, you need to contrive to come across them. Catch Mr Moneybags in transit, especially in wealthy resorts, in luxury hotels and on planes.

Wealthy Holiday Resorts

Casinos, marinas, restaurants and nightclubs are where to find Mr Moneybags once you are in a suitable resort such as Marbella in Spain, Porto di Fino, Forte del Marme or Positano in Italy, Palm Beach or Miami in Florida. There are too many of these resorts to mention all of them but here are a few well known ones to set you on your way.

Monte Carlo is a hive of 'Moneybags', especially at the height of the season in August. There is only the 'right sort of person' here, well-dressed, well-known, and usually emerging from the luxury classic cars such as Aston Martin or Bentley. Wend your way to the casinos. Unless you are wealthy yourself do not dabble in the high stakes but instead reserve your francs for the bar. Become familiar with those around you in the process. Minimum stakes at the six casinos are anything between £5 and £100. But, I repeat, you *don't* have to play all the time!

179

Nice is a favourite playground for the wealthy. A few years ago I roughed it here with my boyfriend and slept on the beach. We left each other for a few hours one morning and arranged to meet up later for lunch. I decided to indulge myself in a big bowl of French coffee in sumptuous surroundings and wandered into a particularly comfortable bar in the centre of town. I couldn't afford a bed, but a bowl of coffee, yes! There weren't many people around as it was mid-morning, but soon a man caught my eye and asked if he could join me. He told me that he had moored his yacht for a few days in Nice because of engine trouble and that he was on his way to a village just beyond Monaco where he had friends. We chatted for a good hour but unfortunately I had to decline his invitation for a drink on the yacht. We had enough in common, not least our good spirits at the beginning of a beautiful new day. Had I not got a prior commitment I would like to have got to know him better!

Deauville in August is reputed to have the greatest concentration of wealth in France. The prestigious horse race meeting, the bloodstock sales, the High Goal polo tournament and American film festival all take place at the same time and draw Mr Moneybags in droves. If you don't meet Mr Moneybags at any of these events during the day, then make the most of the beautiful beach and bide your time to meet him in the evening. Choose the splendid casino perhaps, or one of the countless chic nightclubs and restaurants.

Hotels

A fun challenge is to find a way of using the facilities in a top-class hotel – the swimming pool, bar – without having to pay the phenomenal price of staying there. Call in for a drink, become familiar with the place and then just try your luck. As always, if you are pretty or look the part, you can get away with blue murder. A girlfriend of mine managed to make a few Moneybag contacts through using the Taj Mahal hotel pool in Delhi, while sleeping in the YMCA! Why not try your luck along the same lines in England.

180

Helga, a lively Danish girl, who was fed up with her PA job in the West End of London, decided to seek some excitement in Canada, where she had spent some time as a kid. She had saved up enough money for a few weeks skiing, after which she planned to continue as a skiing instructress for young toddlers. This was not to be, however. During her first week of skiing she had an accident on the slopes. As part of her physiotherapy treatment she was instructed to swim. There were no public pools in the area so this posed a problem. All the hotel pools were restricted to residents, but it didn't stop her from persevering until she found one that would accommodate her. An hotelier of the best hotel in the resort identified with her plight, having suffered a similar skiing accident himself. He generously gave her carte blanche to use the pool, jacuzzi and sauna. Incidentally, it is always best to get hold of people at the top if you can, they are far less petty.

Sitting outside in the bubbling hot jacuzzi under the sun for half of the day, surrounded by snow and getting a tan, was no hardship. People were curious to know about this young woman's circumstances and, unlike the generally reserved English, they didn't hesitate to probe more deeply. In answer to their question, 'You must be really wealthy to stay here,' Helga explained her situation whereupon they would all laugh and chat together. She probably had a lot more to offer the conversation than if she had just been one of the residents!

One day the source of amusement was a Japanese man who persisted in holding a green sponge on top of his head. The conversation went like this:

Him: Where you come from?
Her: London
Him: Ah Rundon England
Her: Where do you come from?
Him: Tokyo. Do you know Tokyo? – he wrings out his sponge – I'm an accantent [accountant] – and puts it back on his head.

181

Her: Aah, interesting, what is the thing on your head?

Him: I know Rundon. Where you stay?

Her: In the north. What is that green sponge on your head for?

At this point a handsome, young man, who turned out to be the son of a shipping magnate, slipped into the jacuzzi with a bottle of wine. He promptly offered her a glass with an expression of amusement. Having little in common with the Japanese she welcomed the distraction, and turned her attention to the newcomer. There was a mutual attraction which led to an exciting three weeks of friendship and romance. The original misfortune of the injury had turned the cards in her favour after all.

Back on home territory, some of the best London hotels serve breakfast from three or four am onwards for those who leave late from chic nightclubs such as Brown's or Stringfellows. People's defences are at a low ebb at this time of the day and meetings are effortless. Consequently, the breakfast rooms of the best hotels would be an appropriate hunting ground for shrewd gold diggers.

Vogue Events

You will find Mr Moneybags at public school open days, wealthy social events such as Royal Ascot in June, Henley Royal Regatta in July, Wimbledon at the end of June, the Glyndbourne Opera Festival in May or the Edinburgh International Festival in August. You will find him at gallery openings, shows and sales at leading auction houses like Bonhams or Christies.

When you are there, arouse your curiosity in a subject that will be of particular interest to him: Ferrari cars at the Motor Show for instance, or the most expensive item in an auction of Persian carpets – the proceeds of which are destined for the estate of some dead multi-billionaire Arab or mega-star.

The next step is to get Mr Moneybags' attention. You are dreaming if you think that *he* will discover *you* as such, so don't hesitate to make yourself known to him. It is self-consciousness or guilt that is the worst enemy of such approaches, so make sure that you are equipped with conviction before you start to operate! Keep your gaze straight, cross him a few times so that he sees you, and then find yourself, for example, musing with him over a picture or an item of sale. It can be done in a subtle way. Practice makes perfect.

In a tent at the Cartier polo tournament in Windsor in July you can be pretty sure that most of the company falls into the Moneybags bracket. Sophie, a comely, well turned out woman, was one of the hostesses here. Her curiosity was aroused by a reserved and very striking-looking African man in a party of five. She passed him a few times and then made eye contact. Having clearly got his attention he found his way over to her – she wasn't too far away! He opened up the conversation with a comment that went beyond the normal bounds of social chit chat, 'I saw you earlier. I'd like to get to know you outside of this situation.' They became friends over the following weeks and ultimately went out with each other. She was not tarty nor was she hard, she was simply genuinely curious to meet him! He turned out to be a well-travelled, international banker over on business from his base in Paris.

Yvonne, an attractive, forty-year-old divorced writer, had taken up some temporary work in the media as she was short of money. She was fed up with doing this kind of work in order to make ends meet so one day she made up her mind to take advantage of an opportunity for the express purpose of meeting a Mr Moneybags. Through work, a free ticket to a press launch of a new interior design company in Chelsea was made available to her. Knowing that it would be full of architects, property developers, high-powered investors and so on, she went along. Her plan worked better than she could possibly have imagined. She walked away with a millionaire Moneybags architect who has kept her in clover ever since.

Maria, a vivacious, English-speaking Italian in her early twenties, found herself at the launch of Joan Collins' new

183

line of jewellery. Maria is involved in fashion promotion and takes a special personal interest in jewellery design; an interest quite easy to develop and by definition likely to attract Mr Moneybags. She knew no-one there except a public relations contact who introduced her to a twenty-nine-year-old press manager called Howard. She wasn't looking for a man, despite the fact that she had not been out with anyone for over a year, so she wasn't feeling shy or self-conscious. After Joan Collins arrived she wandered around with Howard. Her new admirer insisted on joining her for a rendezvous at a bar with her ex-boyfriend afterwards and then taking her out for a meal. Two days later Maria went to Howard's leaving party accompanied by her flatmate. She was too nervous to go on her own. Both of them struck lucky. Her flatmate met her future fiancé, an advertising manager of a smart fashion chronicle, and her own warm feelings towards Howard were confirmed. She was in a perfect situation and in the best frame of mind to meet the love of her life. She describes him as, 'The most interesting man I have ever met – he is humorous, passionate and he's wealthy too!'

Moneybags Activities

Ideally put yourself in a situation where you are doing something alongside Moneybags, such as studying or participating in projects. His defences will be down and there is time to get to know him well. Mr Moneybags commonly gets to know his own privileged order very well in such a way. Why not introduce some new blood? He has repeatedly expressed enthusiasm for this kind of unaffected way of getting to know a woman. As one Mr Moneybags put it, 'It's tiresome to feel that you have to chat a woman up and go through the rigmarole of getting her number, calling her up, arranging dinner and so on.' You can only be admired for your initiative.

Always remember, wealthy doesn't mean snobby. There are many Moneybags people uninterested in the class and position of their friends and associates. People of any background can get up your nose. The beauty of involving yourself in a Moneybags activity is that there is the luxury of time to get to know Mr Moneybags beyond the first impression that he creates. Even if he does swank around with ostentatious labels, or show off about 'Daddy's yacht', there is the time for him to perhaps prove that he is not a boring, unbearable capitalist-pig. You could find that it is just a front.

Try not to ignore the other Moneybags around you when you start to see a lot of one particular Mr Moneybags in any of these natural situations. In other words, don't put all your eggs into one basket or you could end up with no-one. Friends are bad enough when they drop you on finding a new love, but one can usually forgive them. Acquaintances who disappear are generally forgotten!

Honesty and integrity are vital. If you have not got the money to splash out like him, then say so. He will admire your honesty. Anyway, rich people love saying that they are broke themselves, so he will be able to relate to you easily enough! It won't be the fact that you don't have any money that will bother him, it will be if you don't have any conversation.

Operation Raleigh

Many socially aware sons of the wealthy are to be found on an expedition scheme called **Operation Raleigh**. If you are fit, adventurous, between seventeen and twenty-five years old and can spare from ten weeks to three months of your time it is worth a thought. There are executive expeditions for the over twenty-fives as well now. Venturers are chosen on selection weekends, which are apparently run on nearly every weekend of the year. Once you are selected you must raise in the region of £2–3,000 for charity. Of course the more original your idea for raising money – venturers have been known to clean a bus with a toothbrush or to sit in a bath of baked beans for twenty-four hours – the more quickly you are likely to raise it! It cuts across the board socially, and it's a great class leveller.

Arts Appreciation and Wine Courses

The **Arts Appreciation** and **Wine Course** at Sotheby's and Christie's attract those Moneybags who are eager to develop their knowledge in areas of chic investment; added to which there is a high foreign intake. Future career aspirations would be aided by building up a network of friends and contacts from those on the course. For the art courses you will need a few thousand pounds and a year or so free, depending on whether you are doing the part, or full-time course. If you can't afford either of those, then the evening courses are a worthwhile alternative. The wine seminars at Sotheby's for example cost in the region of £220 for a course of five, (or £45 each lesson.).

The wealthy young on these courses are renowned for throwing lavish parties. Hiring some plush nightclub like Tokyo Joe's or Xenon's for a birthday celebration is not uncommon! Take these people as you find them and give 'em a chance gal! Reassure yourself, if you are interested in their life style and the fact that the address list on these courses could sell to *Tatler* magazine, you should have no worries about getting along. After all, your interests and values are similar!

The American College

The **American College** in London is private and expensive but not restricted to Americans. It is a fair assumption that most of the students are well connected through family or friends. With this point in mind it may be worth investing in a business or art-related course for a year or so, maybe on an evening basis, or in a post-graduate degree. It might be a far better investment in the longterm than working your guts out to pay the ever-increasing mortgage rates on an unimpressive house! At least if all else fails, you will have learned something new.

186

Health Farms

Fine for your Sloane Rangers, models and self-indulgent dowagers but what about Miss Normal? Won't she feel a trifle out of place in such lush pleasure grounds? Rest assured, **health farms** attract a broad spectrum of women but a more particular group of men. From cleaning lady to princess, women will go to any amount of expense to improve their looks or beautify themselves. The men who attend are often professionals with highly stressed jobs. They will usually go for health reasons, to counteract the effects of highly pressured lives and too much good living. Stockbrokers, pilots and doctors come into this bracket. Alternatively men go if their well being or looks are important to them for their work, such as professional sportsmen and film and TV actors.

There is time to become acquainted with others in a relaxing environment. As was pointed out to me by an enthusiastic single lady of modest means, the cost of a weekend in a health club represented the sacrifice of only a few evenings out on the town. However, she felt that the 'man capture potential' and the quality of the men available more than compensated for this. Even if you don't meet Mr Moneybags the first time, you won't feel that you have sacrificed anything. You will feel good with that boost to your health, and in better shape to meet interesting men!

Sports Clubs

If you have the money, an expensive sports club is as good a place as any to meet a fine, wealthy man. If you couldn't even conceive of paying the yearly subscription all is not lost. A well-known single mother who I met when she was in her mid-thirties made no bones about how she met a Mr Moneybags through a plush sports club in her locality. She showed interest in joining in order to be given a free invitation to try out the establishment. In the process of 'trying out' the club which she decided not to join, she met and walked away with a ravishing entrepreneur in the motor trade. She is currently spending much of her time doing up a house with him in the South of France.

Charity Work

Charity work in affluent parts of town may create an opportunity to forge a meeting with Mr Moneybags. Lucy, an energetic actress friend of mine, found that she needed to fill in her spare time between performances. Amongst her other activities, she involved herself in charity work. She organised raffles once a week for the mentally handicapped in the wealthy borough of Kensington and Chelsea. Most of the sixteen volunteers she worked with were professionals. Some were involved in public relations, others were in the Moneybags category including one partner of a huge property firm in Hampstead, with whom she now spends the remainder of her spare time.

Motor Clubs

Unless you are a genuine motor enthusiast, motor clubs are going to bore you, so do not even consider anything but the top marques which, I have been reliably informed, are Ferrari, Bentley, Aston Martin, Bugatti and Rolls-Royce. I am also told that an experienced gold digger knows her marques and so will seldom look beyond these five. She is only too aware that many other prestige cars are leased, or are on hire purchase.

The ultimate club for the real gold digger is the Ferrari Owners' Club. It is not necessary to have a Ferrari to turn up at one of the meetings because you can become a member of the associated club for £15 per annum – the **Prancing Horse Register** – and turn up all the same. This enables you to do everything the Ferrari owners do except actually race Ferraris. You can even go Moneybags hunting all over the world through contact Ferrari clubs!

I know of one flirtatious female who slid her tightly-trousered rear into the driving seat of a rare and beautiful Ferrari at one of these club events, having previously got permission from the indulgent owner. Whilst other club members gathered to admire it, believing her to be the owner, they plied her with questions. With immense charm she fibbed convincingly about the car's performance. Inevitably she was invited out by one of them for a drink who, it transpired, was an eligible Testarossa-owner. By the time her deceit was revealed, a new conquest had been made and the fact she didn't own a Ferrari was of no consequence!

You don't have to turn up looking fantastically glamorous, although obviously it helps. What would ensure success would be a knowledge of some of the Ferrari models, so that you can name them. To give yourself excellent credibility develop an interest in cars so that you have some understanding of how they work, how much they cost, and so on. Then focus your interest on sports cars and, in particular, Ferraris. It could be one of the most popular interests you develop, not because it is necessary to be able to talk about Mr Moneybags' greatest toyjoy to be on a par with him, but simply because your common interest encourages conversation and a rapport. I am sure he will be only too delighted to help answer your intelligent questions! There will be a source of conversation for you and Mr Moneybags at your fingertips.

Along the same lines, find work in car sales promotion at a car exhibition such as the Motor Show. You reach Mr Moneybags' attention directly, and flirtation is positively encouraged. Dina, a twenty-five-year-old former theatre technician, got married to an American chain store owner whom she met while promoting Bentley cars. Wendy, a seventeen-year-old model, who was doing promotional work at a private motor show, paused to compliment the young, debonair driver of a Ferrari Spyder, 'You are a lucky man to have such a beautiful car!' This simple line of introduction got her exactly what she wanted – a boyfriend with a Ferrari!

Preferably try to promote the more expensive range of cars. Quite apart from the pick up point, you get a two-day training course on the car before you start. What you learn from this could oil the wheels for future interest in more and more expensive cars!

Association of Self-Employed and Junior Chamber of Commerce

Virtually every large town has a branch of the **Association of**

Self-employed & Small Businesses and a **Junior Chamber of Commerce**. Both these organisations can be a source of rich, eligible young men and it is always worth checking them out because the clubs are very welcoming to potential new members – particularly women.

The Association of the Self-employed is an organisation dedicated to the interests and protection of its members. To anticipate your question, yes it is easy to be self-employed. They don't question too deeply, if at all. After all you might just be thinking of starting your own business!

The Junior Chamber of Commerce is a management training organisation for people from all professions under forty-years-old. However, as with the Federation of the Self-employed, most branches will have a few high flying whizz kids amongst them. It costs in the region of £55 to join and runs a very comprehensive and social programme throughout the year. Many self-employed businessmen on these courses are too isolated in their way of life to meet many women. The Junior Chamber of Commerce in particular puts a high emphasis on social events such as lunches, dinners and dances and therefore can prove a very good venue for meeting enterprising Mr Moneybags. An acquaintance of mine called Rosy, an attractive young nurse, had grown tired of the somewhat cloistered social life in hospital and joined the local Junior Chamber of Commerce. There she met and eventually married a fascinating entrepreneur who owned a chain of popular and trendy wine bars.

Mailing Lists

Put yourself onto a **charity mailing list**. The social events arranged through these are full of well-meaning, wealthy socialites. A fashionable charity like **Birthright** is stuffed with rich people. Anything 'green' is fashionable too, and increasingly popular. Write directly to the charity organisations concerned and asked to be put on their list. Some events you can find advertised in the smarter magazines. Alternatively try to get onto the mailing list of a smart magazine such as *Party Life*, which is aimed at young, successful people and spoilt youngsters. Inside there are invitations to lavish parties which they both organise and advertise. Entry requirements are of the sort that you must arrive in a vintage car – you can always hire one! Tickets for these occasions cost around £26. Contact *Party Life* directly to be put on their mailing list.

First Class Carriages

Invest in a first-class ticket on one of the rush hour trains to towns such as Reading, Horsham or Guildford in the 'Gin and Jag' belt – especially on Friday evening. Invent an aunt there and board it regularly over a few weeks!

Fiona, a polished Fine Arts valuer in her late thirties, frequently buys a second-class ticket and takes a stroll, as though looking for someone she has lost, along the first-class carriage. If a man catches her eye she sits herself down next to him, having apparently given up the search for her lost friend! When the ticket officer comes along she pays the difference, apologises profusely for the fact she has a second-class ticket, saying that she was given the second-class one in error. Many travellers are very bored and only too happy to get involved with an elegant woman served, so to speak, on a plate!

Why not invest in breakfast or a drink in the first-class carriage? There will be plenty of room for friendly glances as you negotiate the problem of sipping from an over-full coffee cup without spilling it all over the object of your desire. This in turn will most likely earn an understanding smile. Gill, a freelance photographer, met and started talking with a well-off divorcee in exactly this way. She spilt her coffee over him in a crowded first-class buffet compartment. For the next few weeks they always went back to the same spot to sit next to each other and chat, in the process building up quite a rapport, which was eventually brought out of the confines of the eleven thirty am from Guildford to London!

Spot The Bachelor

Look out in the evenings for those 'men-shopping-on-their-own' who frequent large supermarkets in affluent areas.

Some supermarkets are so big that you can contrive to bump into him a couple of times and call it an astonishing coincidence. 'We meet again!' Or you can chat to the leather-jacketed Moneybags, tapping his Gucci shoes in impatience in the queue whilst waiting to buy dolcelatte and smoked salmon on the fresh food counter, or indeed whilst waiting in the check-out queues.

Snooty delicatessens of the sort I mentioned in the chapter on the Foreign Type also tend to attract discerning Mr Moneybags of class, and also greed, who are spoiling for bachelor self indulgence! Try Partridges on Sloane Street. The clientele's bank balances there must add up at any one time to a few million. Or if you are ever in Los Angeles, pay a visit to their Singles Safeways and pick up a Moneybags there at key times of the day. Generally the Americans are interested in the English so you will have an advantage over all the other women wheeling their singles trolleys around!

Making it Together

You may of course meet your entrepreneur before he makes his money. If it is his strength of character or charm that attracts you most, then whether he is successful in business or not may not be so important. However, if money is the criterion which attracts you then you are taking a gamble in getting involved with him, and you have to assess the likelihood of his success. Ask yourself the question, 'Is he a stayer or is he a butterfly?' As a general rule successful entrepreneurs will lock on to an idea and bulldoze their way through all obstacles until they achieve success. This major characteristic separates the many would-be-entrepeneurs from the real thing. Take a hard look at him and ask yourself whether you see him doing this. If you do, go for it!

Advertising

Advertising in a newspaper or magazine with a wealthy readership is a popular route used by Mr Moneybags to find a partner. Due to his workaholic tendencies he often finds himself grounded in the relationship stakes. Remember, should you be tempted to reply, that you are approaching a personal matter in a logical, businesslike way and 'meeting' is as far as the ad can take you. Thereafter you and he are on your own, without the aid of professional props. You will need to cultivate a friendship – or whatever – with time. Beauty is obviously an advantage, but never forget that beauty is in the eye of the beholder. Fortunately, it can appear in many guises. Some prefer brunettes whilst others prefer blondes, others hanker after the statuesque whilst many prefer the petite. Some just don't care! Most humans have a few outstanding points, whether physically or mentally. We are all different in our requirements so don't put yourself down before you have even started.

When it comes to putting ads in newspaper columns for companionship and romance women usually get a far greater response from men than men do from women. Among the genuinely interested replies from men there are bound to be some which suggest that 'You are just dying for it!'. Ignore them. It is up to you to sort through them. Men don't get so much response partly because they are hopeless at presenting themselves. Often they don't seem to have a clue of what a woman wants in a man, or maybe they can't comprehend!

Once you have sorted out the ads that interest you, use the telephone to gauge whether they are worthwhile following up, although always beware of the safety aspect, ie, don't give him your phone number or address if you are living alone – find another way of contact.

Market Research

Be discerning about where you place your ad and about where you reply to an ad. I, for instance, inadvertently met a wealthy entrepreneur through answering an ad in the window of a newsagent in Sloane Square – an example of a good position for an ad if ever there was one! In return for living rent-free in his Chelsea home, he wanted help in setting up his health-food business. We hit it off so well on the telephone that we became friends before we had even met. Although the original plan fell through, our friendship has continued.

In the back of a magazine like *Time Out* an ad can get lost amongst the jamboree. In a magazine which hits an affluent market such as *Harpers & Queen, Ritz* magazine, or the Wednesday and Saturday rendezvous pages of *The Times*, you should reach the right sort of person directly. I mean the sort of person who can afford to make appropriate overtures, like these two Moneybags: one sent a bouquet of flowers to the lady before he had even seen her and then treated her to a champagne lunch at the Royal Garden Hotel! Another arranged for a limousine to collect the lady in question for a proper introduction at Royal Ascot!

A good ploy is to put an ad in the back of a polo, yachting, farming or aeroplane magazine, in other words a Moneybags leisure magazine. You won't know until you have given yourself the opportunity to develop such an interest whether it turns you on or not. Try something new. I thought I would be bored stiff with the motor racing crowd but I found them exciting, very switched on, and fun to be with. At least none of them were likely to slope into a sedentary life style. No matter which privileged leisure activity you choose to look into you will be brought into contact with Mr Moneybags either directly, or through his connections with the in-crowd!

I interviewed a man called Roger who had set up a multi-million pound electronic engineering company. Unfortunately for him, all the work and time it entailed had cost him his social life. As a consequence he decided to give **Singles Magazine** a try. This is a journal aimed at a cross section of people and divided into two sections – one for men and one for women in which to put their respective ads with a box number. After several unsuccessful rendezvous he wrote to a woman on the strength of her amusing ad which had caught his attention. Later on, speaking to each other on the phone, they hit it off straight away. More than anything else it was their similar sense of humour which attracted them to one another. She was a single parent with a kid, and on the dole. As a result of their relationship she became pregnant and blessed them with twins! He didn't want to commit himself to marriage but he decided to reorganise his life so as to help her raise the children. He spends three days a week looking after the children and the rest involving himself in business interests.

Housekeeper

Another successful way of alighting on a rich nest is either to advertise yourself as, or reply to, an ad for the post of housekeeper. Again it is best to use a journal aimed at capturing the Moneybags readership. This is an effective route for many women into fresh and glamorous social circles. Frequently it leads to marriage, although not necessarily with the man whose house they move into!

Julie, an ex-fashion buyer who had grown tired of her occupation, answered a job advertised in the *Lady* magazine for a housekeeper and moved in with a solicitor of great family wealth. He had a country mansion near Cheltenham, tennis courts, horses, swimming pool and so on. She cherished him in the hope that he might ask her to marry him. He, never having had it so good, made no proposal. One day she threatened him, 'If you don't marry me I'll marry the first man that asks me,' but he didn't take any notice. She was whisked off the next day to Cheltenham races by a civil engineer whom she had met at one of the solicitor's dinner parties. Having spotted what an altogether suitable and wonderful woman she was, a marriage deal was clinched between his proposal during the two o'clock and her acceptance during the three thirty race that afternoon!

A millionaire commodity broker, looking for a housekeeper, rather ineptly jumped the gun and proposed on the strength of numerous telephone calls with Clara, a single mother in her mid-thirties who was interested in the position. They met at Tramp nightclub, but one look at the enormous wadge of fat spilling over the top of his trousers, together with the balding head and sweaty handshake and she realised that Saville Row shirt, Gucci belt and Lamborghini car aside, he was not for her. However, she wasn't deterred from trying again, and the next time she replied to an ad in *The Times* advertising for a housekeeper she was successful. She met an Old Etonian who had slipped out of the city rat race to celebrate life through wine, women and song. She duly married him and has to all intents and purposes cured him of his weakness for conquering women and drinking. Several hours are passed each day on the phone to the London stock market from their comfortable villa they are now doing up near Barcelona.

Handy Hints

Rich Foreigners
If you want to meet someone who is simply rich, then angle for a rich foreigner. He might well be your best bet. Remember that he is unlikely to be preoccupied with your background or circumstances. Depending on the country, foreign men are on the whole likely to spoil you deliciously as well.

Don't be Impressed
When Mr Moneybags invites you back to his plush residence, whether it be a yacht, a palace or a penthouse apartment overlooking Eaton Square, try not to look as though you are impressed. Sit down on the silk and gold threaded divan as though you are on your own living room sofa. Comment pleasantly on a little picture or artefact in the room. It is only polite to make some positive allusion if you are invited to somebody's house, but he will have to work a little harder if he wants to seduce you. Evidently, you are used to this scene . . . and not an impressionable walk over, like so many of the other girls you can imagine he has brought back!

Keeping the Balance
Keep up a delicate and exciting balance of distance but at the same time obvious interest. As Valmont puts it in *Les Liaisons Dangereuses*, 'The real intoxication: when you know

she loves you, but you're still not quite certain of victory.' Those women that are available to go out, but are not an easy lay (commonly known as a *p.t*), usually get the best deal! It is a woman's prerogative to say no at this stage of the game! So if you are interested in him, see him a lot, flirt, but don't succumb to his charm until you know him well.

Always Insist on the Best
Set a good precedent at the beginning and always insist on the best. Be presumptuous but at all times well mannered. If he wants to play rich then he had better do it properly or you are not interested. He will use a great deal of his resources to impress and lure a woman — weekends in Paris, nights at Annabel's, invitations to balls and so on.

Pearl, a chic and outgoing twenty-two-year-old, had no qualms about manipulating some Moneybags Sloanies to take her and her friend out for the evening. They met at a fashionable wine bar in Chelsea called The Pheasantry where the two women insisted on drinking nothing but champagne at the Sloanies' expense. They then moved on to an expensive club, and continued to drink champagne until the club closed. Breakfast at the Ritz Hotel rounded off the evening in suitable style, thank you very much. How did she do it? With style and nerve!

Continue to be Flirtatious
Be flirtatious with everyone around you to keep him on his toes. Continue your romantic friendships. Never let go. In the same way as it is apparently a turn-on to know that a man has had strings of girls and that girls are always interested in him, Mr Moneybags will feel reassured if he knows that he is with someone of value, measured by the attention you are receiving. Do not, however, overstep the mark because you could upset the apple cart and lose him!

Reassure Him of Your Love
Mr Moneybags needs reassurance. Some advice from a sophisticated and worldly woman I interviewed was, 'Be

affectionate and tell him that you love him, give him credit where it's due, see him a lot. Altogether, get his trust and then cool off, by which time he will have given too much of himself to want to pull out. It is always good for the ego to have gone out with the guy you wanted and then to be strong enough to be able to demand more of him. You are perceived as a "hard woman to please" and "awfully chic", and if he's unco-operative you can discard him!' In reality it is because you have realised your fantasy that you become discontented and ambitious all over again!

Basic Business Terms

Make yourself aware of basic business terms. If you understand the vocabulary of the man's world – stocks and shares, company structure and so on – you will soar in his estimation and he won't be in a position to patronise you. One of my interviewees, a very young and successful entrepreneur, was going through a complicated court case which he was in the process of losing. He alluded to it but he didn't elaborate upon it until he heard that I had a law degree. 'Oh, I didn't realize you were so intelligent,' he said. From that point on he opened up, relating to me with enthusiasm exactly what was happening. I had no more to say than anyone without a law degree but in his mind the fact that I had a grasp of law terms put us on a level and opened up the male/female dividing line.

Business matters are frequently on Mr Moneybags' mind. It would be good for him if you could lend a sympathetic ear now and again. Try to avoid being excluded from conversation through ignorance, or rather, lack of interest. Fair enough, he is not necessarily going to want to talk about business socially, but it is better in general for relationships if he can at least allude to what is on his mind from time to time.

Should you marry such a man, and later divorce him, he won't be able to pull the wool over your eyes. Your constant interest in his affairs will have kept you up to date as to what he is worth. Why do you think I interested myself in law? To set me up with some understanding of the legal world, so that

I wouldn't be completely duped by it! I would never want anything like the following situation to happen to me.

A woman met her husband's first wife – the mother of his twins – and stated, 'The thing that most turned me on about Sam was his money. He is always very generous to me. I don't think you have any idea of exactly how wealthy your kids are going to be one day . . .' Wife number one had not put up any fight at the divorce settlement because she honestly believed that what he was offering to pay was all he could manage. She has been left with a very modest settlement on which you can only say she struggles to bring up the children.

It came through clearly in the interviews I conducted that the more that men and women have an appreciation of each other's lives the more respect that there is between them and the closer it brings them together. Judging from the enthusiasm they showed, the Moneybags men in particular would appreciate being challenged and heard with understanding on a few more issues.

Don't Put Yourself Down

When Mr Moneybags asks you what you do, avoid putting yourself down like this: 'Oh, nothing very interesting, I'm just working in a shop,' or 'I'm a temp,' or 'I'm a secretary,' because that will fall rather flat. Put yourself in a fair light so that he can pick up on a point of interest, 'Well, I'm temping at the moment but what I really do is design hats,' as the girl in the film *Slaves of New York* put it, 'And to get that under way I need some money.' Or, like some one I know, 'I'm writing a book but in order to keep myself alive I'm working under the eye of an alcoholic, misogynist restaurateur as a waitress. It's fun to have done but it's the sort of thing you don't want to go back to if you can help it!' Or 'I'm at present helping in a shop which I quite enjoy. Later on, when I've solved a few financial problems and learnt Spanish, which I am at present studying, I hope to become a stewardess/to set up an export import business in textiles,' etc . . . If you don't have any aspirations but are working for an interesting or well-known company, then throw that iron into the fire for conversation!

Payment Rules
Don't be presumptuous over payment of the bill in a restaurant, or about paying for theatre tickets and so on, particularly if he is around your own age and you are working. Firstly, Mr Moneybags likes to be reassured that you are not after his money, even though it is perhaps little more than a token gesture. Secondly, it gives you a chance to thank him for his generosity, and to build up his ego. It is not always easy to say thank you, but it is well worth learning how to say it all the same.

Appreciate Money
I am afraid the only solution is 'If you can't beat him, join him,' and share his lust for the acquisition of assets and the appraisal of their worth, now, then, and in the future. It can only enrich conversation! I knew of one millionaire's family where the parents used to do the accounts seriously every Friday evening, down to every single penny, such as the cost of the white sliced loaf, and the number of tins of baked beans they were going to leave their fourteen-year-old son for the weekend. The marriage worked terribly well because they both thought in exactly the same way and lived in splendid control!

Be Careful With His Toys
He is likely to be overprotective about his expensive toys. For example, don't try and operate his hi-fi equipment if you can't, because you'll irritate him beyond belief if you damage it. Mr Moneybags is a precious toy as well, so he needs careful handling too!

Final Word

So, as you have read, you can literally meet any man who takes your fancy or your fantasy! You are not a sitting duck. You are a bright chick who recognises the power of being a woman and who uses her initiative. This book is about looking beyond yourself and endeavouring to meet and understand interesting men. I hope that it will help to bring some of the lonely women, who are pining to meet a few interesting men, out of their shells and into the open. I hope that it will inspire and show other more outgoing women where to go to meet more new and interesting men. Two of the most important points I'd like to emerge from this book are that women are far more in control of their lives than they think and that they are welcome to come forward and make themselves known to men without feeling ashamed or being branded tarts. Now those points are cleared up and you know where to go it is up to you to meet whoever tickles your fancy! I can guarantee that you will have a lot of fun trying!

List of Addresses

Chapter One: The Outdoor Type

Aircraft Owners & Pilots Association, 50a Cambridge Street, London SW1V 4QQ   *Tel* 071 834 5631

Bladon Lines Travel Ltd, 56 Putney High Street, London SW15 1SF   *Tel* 081 785 3131

British Ballooning and Airship Club, Information Officer, PO Box 1006, Birmingham BS 5RT   *Tel* 021 643 3224

British Canoe Union, Mapperley Hall, Lucknow Avenue, Nottingham NG3 5FA   *Tel* 0602 821100

British Hang-gliding Association, Cranfield Airfield, Cranfield, Bedford MK43 0YR   *Tel* 0234 751344

British Microlight Aircraft Association, The Bull ring, Deddington, Banbury, Oxford OX15 0TT   *Tel* 0869 38888

British Parachuting Association, Wharf Way, Glenpava, Leicester LE2 9TF   *Tel* 0533 785271

British Trust for Conservation Volunteers (BTCV), 36 St Mary Street, Wallington, Oxfordshire OX10 0EU   *Tel* 0491 397766

Capital Balloon Club/Ballooning World, 18 Lindhope Street, London NW1 6HT   *Tel* 071 706 1021

Club Mediterranee (UK) Ltd, 106 Brompton Road, London SW3 1JJ   *Tel* 071 581 1161

Commonwealth Veterinary Association, Miss H Steed, BVNA Overseas Liaison, Royal Veterinary College, Queen Mother Hospital, Hawkeshead Lane, North Mymms, Hatfield, Herts AL9 7TA   *Tel* 0707 55486

Cowes Tourist Information Centre, The Arcade, Fountain Key, Cowes, Isle of Wight PO31 7AR   *Tel* 0983 291914

Cross Keys public house, Cusco, Peru

Expeditionary Advisory Service, 1 Kensington Gore, London SW7 2AR   *Tel* 071 581 2057

Farmers Weekly Magazine, Greenfield House, 69–73 Manor Road, Wallington, Surrey SM6 0DX   *Tel* 081 661 4911

Flypast magazine, P.O. Box 100, Stamford, Lincs. PE9 1XQ   *Tel* 0780 55131

Horse and Hound Magazine, Kings Reach Tower, Stamford Street, London SE1 9LS   *Tel* 071 261 6315

Horses in Training published by Raceform Ltd, Compton, Newbury, Berks RG16 7BR   *Tel* 0635 578080 Published annually, £10.95 from bookshops or £11.50 including postage and packaging on subscription.

Job Directory of Voluntary Work, published by Vacation Work, 9 Park End Street, Oxford OX1 1HJ   *Tel* 0865 241978/243311

Land-Rover Owners International (LRO) published by The Hollies, Botesdale, Diss, Norfolk IP22 1BZ   *Tel* 0379 890056 £1.75 monthly

Mayhem Wargames Ltd, Sunset Farm, Cross-In-Hand, Heathfield, East Sussex TN21 0IX   *Tel* 0435 866189

The National Trust, 36 Queen Anne's Gate, London SW1 H9AS   *Tel* 071 222 9251

Overseas Jobs and Working Holidays, Job Search, Broads Lane, Mylor, Falmouth, Cornwall (Monthly information service, include two first-class stamps when writing)

Pilot Magazine, 88 Burlington Road, New Malden, Surrey KT3 4NT   *Tel* 081 949 3642

Royal Geographic Society, 1 Kensington Gore, London SW7 2AR   *Tel* 071 589 2173

Royal Yacht Association (RYA), Romsey Road, Eastleigh, Hants SO5 4YA   *Tel* 0703 629962

Summer Jobs Abroad, Vacation Work, 9 Part End Street, Oxford OX1 1HJ   *Tel* 0865 241978/243311

The Tiger Club, Headcorn Aerodrome, Ashford, Kent TN29 9HK   *Tel* 0622 891017

TNT Couriers, 346 Fulham Road, London SW10 9UH   *Tel* 071 351 0300

Worldwide Fund for Nature UK and International, Panda House, Weyside, Cattershall Lane, Godalming, Surrey GU17 1W3   *Tel* 0483 426444

Charity Organisations

Conservation Trust, The George Palmer Site, Northumberland Avenue, Reading, Berks RG2 7PW   *Tel* 0734 868442 (Acts as a data information system for outdoor charities.)

Intermediate Technological Development Group (ITDG), Myson House, Railway Terrace, Rugby CB21 3HT   *Tel* 0788 60631

Woodland Trust, Autumn Park, Grantham, Lincolnshire NG31
6LL   *Tel* 0476 74297
Working Weekends on Organic Farms, 19 Bedford Road, Lewes,
East Sussex BN7 1RB   *Tel* 0273 476286

Agricultural Colleges

Askham Bryan College of Agriculture and Horticulture, Askham
Bryan, York YR2 3PB   *Tel* 0904 702121
Cirencester Royal Agriculture College, Strand Road, Cirencester,
Gloucestershire GL7 6JS   *Tel* 0285 652531
Harper Adams Agricultural College, Newport, Shropshire TF10
8NB   *Tel* 0952 820280
Seale Hayne Agricultural College, Newton Abbott, Devon TQ12
6OQ   *Tel* 0626 52323
Writtle College, Chelmsford, Essex CM1 3RR   *Tel* 0245 420705
Wye College, University of London, Ashford, Kent TN25
5AH   *Tel* 0233 812401
Young Farmers Club, National Agricultural Centre, Kennilworth,
Warwicks CV8 2LE   *Tel* 0203 696544

Chapter Two: The Intellectual Type

British Council for Archeology, 112 Kennington Road, London
SW11 6RE   *Tel* 071 582 0494

Chapter Three: The Foreign Type

Au pair Contact, 50 Ullswater Road, Barnes SW13 9PN   *Tel* 081
748 2657
Au pairs, The Britannia Agency, EBC House, Richmond Street
Buildings, Kew Road, Richmond, Surrey TW9 2NA   *Tel* 081
332 1404
British Red Cross Society, 9 Grosvenor Crescent, London SW1X
7EJ   *Tel* 071 235 5454
Kibbutz Representatives, 1a Accommodation Road, London
NW11 8ED   *Tel* 081 458 9235
RSA English as a Foreign Language Division, 1 Hills Road,
Cambridge CB1 2EU   *Tel* 0223 61111
TEFL Teacher Training Department, International House, 106
Piccadilly, London W1V 9EL   *Tel* 071 491 2598
Voluntary Service Overseas, 317 Putney Bridge Road, London
SW15 2PN   *Tel* 081 780 2266

Chapter Four: The Film and Advertising Type

Association of Model Agents, 6 St Catherine's Mews, London
SW3 2PX   *Tel* 071 584 6466

Design and Art Direction, Nash House, 12 Carlton House
Terrace, London SW1Y 5AH   *Tel* 071 839 2964/5

Norrie Carr (child agent), 30 Fryent Way, London SW9 9SB   *Tel*
081 204 2241

Pathfinders, 32 Maddox Street, London W1R 9PF   *Tel* 071
629 3132

Ugly Enterprises (character/lookalike specialist modelling),
Tigris House, 256 Edgware Road, London W2 1DS   *Tel* 071
402 5564

Chapter Five: The Sporty Type

Amateur Fencing Association, 83 Perham Road, West
Kensington, London W14 9SP   *Tel* 071 385 7442

Autosport magazine, Autosport Subscription Dept., Haymarket
Magazines Ltd; 12–14 Ansdell Street, London W8   *Tel* 071
938 0788

Cowdray Park Polo Club, Estate Office, Midhurst, W. Sussex
GU29 0AQ   *Tel* 0730 813257

Guards Polo Club, Windsor Great Park, Englefield Green, Egham,
Surrey TW20 0HP   *Tel* 0784 437797

Horses in Training (see address in Chapter One address section
above)

Marshalls Club (see Motor Sports Association below)

Motoring News Magazine, News Publications Ltd., Standard
House, Bonhill Street, London EC2A 4DA   *Tel* 04 628 4741

Motor Sport Directory (see RAC Motor Sports Association below)

National Softball Federation, PO Box 1303, London NW3 5TU

RAC Motor Sports Association Ltd, Motor Sports House,
Riverside Park, Colnbrook, Slough SL3 0HG   *Tel* 0753 681736

Professional Golfing Association, Apollo House, The Belfry,
Sutton Coldfield, West Midlands B76 9BT   *Tel* 0675 470333

Sun Living, 10 Milton Court, Ravenshead, Nottingham NG15
9BD   *Tel* 0623 795365 (24 hrs)

Chapter Six: The Arty Type

Aldeburgh Foundation, High Street Aldeburgh, Suffolk IP15
5AX   *Tel* 0728 453543

Artists Newsletter, Arctic Producers, PO Box 23, Sunderland SR4 6DG *Tel* 091 567 3589

Art Monthly, 36 Great Russell Street, London WC1 3PP *Tel* 071 581 4168

Bath Festival, Linley House, Pierrepont Place, Bath BA1 1JY *Tel* 0225 462231

British Interior Design Exhibition, 107a Pimlico Road, London SW1W 8PH *Tel* 071 730 2353

British Film Institute, 21 Stephens Street, London W1 *Tel* 071 255 1444

The Caterer & Hotel Keeper, Reed Business Publishing Group, Quadrant House, The Quadrant, Sutton, Surrey SM2 5AS *Tel* 081 661 3500

Cheltenham Festival of Literature, Cheltenham Town Hall, Imperial Square, Cheltenham, Gloucestershire GL50 1QA *Tel* 0242 521621

Classical Music Magazine, Rhinegold Publishing, 241 Shaftesbury Avenue, London WC2H 8EH *Tel* 071 836 2383/2534

The Creative Handbook, British Media Publications, Windsor Court, East Grinstead House, East Grinstead, W. Sussex RH19 1XA *Tel* 0342 326972

The White Book, The International Production Directory, Birdhurst Ltd., PO Box 551, Staines, Middlesex TW18 4UG *Tel* 0784 464 441

Edinburgh International Festival, 21 Market Street, Edinburgh, Scotland *Tel* 031 226 4001

Edinburgh Fringe Festival, 180 High Street, Edinburgh, Scotland *Tel* 031 226 5257

Glyndebourne Opera Festival, Box Office, Glyndebourne, Lewes, East Sussex BN8 SUU *Tel* 0273 541111

The Knowledge, P.A. Publishing Co. Ltd., Unit 3, The Grand Union Centre, West Row, London W10 5AS *Tel* 081 969 5777

Chapter Seven: The Professional Type

Amnesty International, 1 Easton Street, London WC1X 8DJ *Tel* 071 413 5500

Architectural Association, 36 Bedford Square, London WC1B 3ES *Tel* 071 636 0974

British Chess Federation, La Grand Parade, St Leonards-on-Sea, East Sussex *Tel* 0424 442500

Charity Organisations: see Chapter Nine, below.

Haldane Society of Socialist Lawyers, Room 205, Panther House, 38 Mount Pleasant, London WC1X 0AP *Tel* 071 833 8958

English Bridge Union, Broadfields, Bicester Road, Aylesbury
Bucks HP19 3BG   *Tel* 0296 394414
National Council of Civil Liberties, 21 Tabard Street, London
SE1 4LA   *Tel* 071 403 3888

Chapter Eight: Travel Tips

Youth Hostel Association, 8 St Stephens Hill, St Albans, Herts
AL1 2DY   *Tel* 0727 55215

Chapter Nine: Gold Diggers Anonymous

The American College, 110 Marylebone High Street, London
W1M 3DB   *Tel* 071 486 1772
Association of the Self Employed, 33 The Green, Kalne,
Wiltshire SN11 8DJ   *Tel* 0249 814908
British Junior Chamber of Commerce, 12 Regent Place, Rugby,
Warwickshire CV21 2PN   *Tel* 0788 572795
Champneys Health Farm, Tring, Herts HP23 6HY   *Tel* 0442
873155
Christies Education Department, 85 Old Brompton Road,
London SW7 3JS   *Tel* 071 581 3933
Henlow Grange Health Farm, Henlow, Bedfordshire   *Tel* 0462
811111
Operation Raleigh, Alpha Place, Flood Street, London SW3
5SZ   *Tel* 071 351 7541
Prancing Horse Register, Ray Jenkins, 30 Temple Grove, Barkers
Lane, West Hanningfield, Chelmsford, Essex CM2 8LQ   *Tel*
0533 303657
Sotheby's Educational Studies, 30 Oxford Street, London W1R
1RE   *Tel* 071 323 5775
Sotheby's Wine Department, 5 Albion Wharf, Hester Road,
London SW11 4AN   *Tel* 071 924 3287

Other Charity Organisations

International Fund for Animal Welfare, 35 Boundary Road,
London W8 0JE   *Tel* 071 624 3535
The Appeals Dept, Royal Society for Mentally Handicapped
Children and Adults (MENCAP), Mencap National Centre, 123
Golden Lane, London EC1 YORT   *Tel* 071 454 0454
MIND, 22 Harley Street, London W1N 2ED   *Tel* 071 242 1626
NSPCC, 67 Saffron Hill, London EC1N 8RS   *Tel* 071 242 1626

Oxfam, 274 Banbury Road, Oxford OX2 7DZ   *Tel* 0865 56777
Whale and Dolphin Conservation Society, 20, West Lea Road,
   Bath, Avon BA1 3RL   *Tel* 0225 334511

Mailing Lists

Association of Business Sponsorship of the Arts, 2 Chester
   Street, London SW1X 7BB   *Tel* 071 235 9781
Birthright Childbirth Research Fund, 27 Sussex Place, Regent's
   Park London NW1 4SP   *Tel* 071 723 9296/262 5337/402 6407
Charities Aid Foundation, 48 Pembury Road, Tunbridge TN9
   2JD   *Tel* 0732 771333
Help the Aged, St James Walk, London EC1 0BE   *Tel* 071
   253 0253
Party Life magazine, 13 Knightsbridge Green, Knightsbridge,
   London SW1X 7QL   *Tel* 071 384 1767
Save the Children Fund, Mary Datchelor House, 17 Grove Lane,
   London SE5 8RD   *Tel* 071 703 5400
Singles magazine, 23 Abingdon Road, London W8 6AH   *Tel* 071
   938 1011
The Prince's Trust, 8 Bedford Row, London WC1R 4BU   *Tel* 071
   430 0527

HEATHER FORMAINI

Men: The Darker Continent

Why are men so fearful of intimacy and commitment? Why are they so often inadequate as husbands and fathers? Is masculinity simply a process of societal conditioning?

Two decades of feminism have compelled women to question their place in a man's world. Now, a practising psychoanalyst turns the spotlight on men, and on the darkest corners of the male psyche. Heather Formaini's analysis is disturbing and controversial.

'This is a book about the tryanny of masculinity, the martial law imposed by manhood, the lives and crimes of men – the prisoners of gender' Tony Parsons, *Guardian*

'Neatly reverses Freud's image of women as unexplored, unexplorable terrain. . . Far from viewing men as an enigma, Formaini has firm ideas about them and what is wrong with them. Her book is an attempt to track down the roots of their misogyny, their fear of intimacy, and their violence to women' Joan Smith

'So illuminating that I found myself reading bits of it onto a friend's answerphone' *Independent*

ANNE MOIR & DAVID JESSEL

Brainsex

What makes men succeed in one profession —
women in another? Is there such a thing as
female intuition? Why does man so often find
woman a mystery? Are men as promiscuous as
women claim? If so, why are women so good
at finding them out?

Are the differences more than skin deep?

Happily of different sex, the authors of this
stimulating and controversial book at last answer
the questions that continue to inflame a time-
honoured debate. *BrainSex* is a radical rethink of
conventional wisdom. Because the brain is sexed
in the womb.

It is futile, therefore, as Moir and Jessel
provocatively and authoritatively point out,
to maintain that the sexes are interchangeable.
In the classroom, bedroom or boardroom, boys
will be boys. And the girls will not. Indispensable to both sexes, this book is a celebration of
difference.

'This book is a thoroughly good read, couched
comfortably in layman's language and carrying
the reader on at a spanking pace' *Glasgow
Herald*

'For the past 30 years we have been told
that men and women are interchangeable in
every way. Now a sensational book explodes
the myth of sexual sameness' *Daily Mail*

A Selected List of Non-Fiction Available from Mandarin

While every effort is made to keep prices low, it is sometimes necessary to increase prices at short notice. Mandarin Paperbacks reserves the right to show new retail prices on covers which may differ from those previously advertised in the text or elsewhere.

The prices shown below were correct at the time of going to press.

☐ 7493 0109 0	**The Warrior Queens**	Antonia Fraser	£4.99
☐ 7493 0108 2	**Mary Queen of Scots**	Antonia Fraser	£5.99
☐ 7493 0010 8	**Cromwell**	Antonia Fraser	£7.50
☐ 7493 0106 6	**The Weaker Vessel**	Antonia Fraser	£5.99
☐ 7493 0014 0	**The Demon Drink**	Jancis Robinson	£4.99
☐ 7493 0016 7	**Vietnam – The 10,000 Day War**	Michael Maclear	£3.99
☐ 7493 0061 2	**Voyager**	Yeager/Rutan	£3.99
☐ 7493 0113 9	**Peggy Ashcroft**	Michael Billington	£3.99
☐ 7493 0177 5	**The Troubles**	Mick O'Connor	£4.99
☐ 7493 0004 3	**South Africa**	Graham Leach	£3.99
☐ 7493 0254 2	**Families and How to Survive Them**	Creese/Skynner	£5.99
☐ 7493 0060 4	**The Fashion Conspiracy**	Nicolas Coleridge	£3.99
☐ 7493 0179 1	**The Tao of Pooh**	Benjamin Hoff	£2.99
☐ 7493 0000 0	**Moonwalk**	Michael Jackson	£2.99

All these books are available at your bookshop or newsagent, or can be ordered direct from the publisher. Just tick the titles you want and fill in the form below.

Mandarin Paperbacks, Cash Sales Department, PO Box 11, Falmouth, Cornwall TR10 9EN.

Please send cheque or postal order, no currency, for purchase price quoted and allow the following for postage and packing:

UK   80p for the first book, 20p for each additional book ordered to a maximum charge of £2.00.

BFPO   80p for the first book, 20p for each additional book.

Overseas   £1.50 for the first book, £1.00 for the second and 30p for each additional book
including Eire   thereafter.

NAME (Block letters) ....

ADDRESS ....

....

....